Greek Mythology

From Aphrodite to Zeus - The Gods, Goddesses, Heroes, and Monsters of Ancient Greece

By History Activist Readers

Introduction

Do you love Greek mythology?

If you're a fan of Greek mythology, then this is the book for you. It contains everything from the creation of the world to the death of Olympus. You'll learn about all the major gods and goddesses, as well as dozens of lesser-known characters. This is an essential guide for any mythology lover, a comprehensive guide to all the gods, goddesses, heroes and monsters of Ancient Greece.

The stories of ancient Greece are some of the most famous in all of mythology. For thousands of years, people have been fascinated by the gods and goddesses, heroes, and monsters of Greek mythology. The stories were originally passed down orally, and only later were they written down. Many of the stories were eventually collected in a book called The Iliad, which was written by the poet Homer. Other popular Greek myths include The Odyssey, The Argonautica, and The Argonauts.

These stories tell of the great adventures of heroes like Hercules and Jason, as they journeyed to far-off lands in search of adventure and danger. Along the way, they would encounter fantastic creatures like the Minotaur and the Hydra, as well as beautiful goddesses like Aphrodite and Athena.

While the stories are full of adventure, they also teach important lessons about morality, courage, and loyalty. With gripping storytelling, this book brings ancient Greece to life like never before. Experience Greek mythology like never before with this must-read book. You'll be entranced by their stories and amazed at the power they wielded over mortals and gods alike.

Table of Content

Greek Mythology

Greek mythology is the body of ancient Greek myths and sagas. These are stories about gods, demigods and contact between gods and humans.

Greek mythology gave the ancient Greeks explanations for the origin of the world, the heavenly bodies, people, gods, evil, diseases, natural phenomena and the primal elements of earth, water, fire and air. It formed the basis of the religion of the ancient Greeks. They are known to have made attempts to systematize and reshape known myths from their own culture and environment, making extensive use of etiology and eponymy. This involved establishing family trees of known gods and mythical beings. Older deities, sometimes from other cultures such as Anatolia, ancient Mesopotamia and Egypt, were incorporated and fitted in, and new myths were created to explain such fitting in. Old almost forgotten historical events were also elevated to myth (such as that of the Amazons) or were handed down in myth form. As a result, mythology in general took on a renewed appearance and became very extensive and very complex.

Polytheism

The Greeks believed that there were many different gods and other mythical beings, most of whom were demigods. They were thus polytheistic (*poly* = many and *theos* = god) and worshiped a *pantheon* of gods and goddesses. Part of the reason for this polytheism is that many local cults were united into one pan-Hellenic religion, as was the case with Egyptian mythology. The stories of the gods were handed down orally, which is probably why local variations and contradictory facts appear here and there.

In the Greek world, sacrifices were made to propitiate or thank the gods. This was often done on an altar. Such an altar stood in a *temenos*, a sacred domain, which sometimes included a temple. A sacrifice was often an agricultural product; a blood donation was usually a (healthy) animal. Myths do tell of human sacrifice, such as the story in which Agamemnon sacrifices his daughter Iphiginea in order to obtain from Artemis a favorable wind to sail to Troy.

The Greek gods possessed extraordinary powers, but could assume human forms and displayed human behavior and flaws. Power games were often played, and emotions such as lust, anger, mirth and jealousy were not foreign to them.

Celebrations

Important events, such as agricultural festivals, were celebrated with ritual games, the singing of songs and with special parades, often wearing masks of gods. This is especially true of the cult of Dionysus, the god of wine, intoxication and a bit of agriculture. From these masked parades later emerged the Greek tragedies and comedies. When important decisions had to be made, people often asked for advice. People went to the temple at Delphi to ask for an oracle, an advisory pronouncement from the gods.

Such an oracle, partly by cloaking himself in vague statements and partly by great political knowledge, could make surprisingly good predictions.

Expressions

Many terms and expressions in contemporary language are derived from Greek mythology. Examples include a tantalus affliction, Pandora's box, a sisyphean labor, the Achilles' heel, an Oedipus complex, an electra complex, an augias stable, an Achilles' heel, an odyssey, a muse and an oracle (spell). Many planets, stars and other celestial bodies also bear names from Greek mythology.

Stories

Some of the stories, such as the one about an all-consuming flood, are found in other mythological and belief systems. Both the Tanakh/Old Testament and Plato tell of a "flood. Very early myths from Mesopotamian mythology also make mention of such an occurrence. One possible explanation is that such an event did indeed occur and took various forms through oral tradition. See also Greek flood stories and origins of humanity in Greek mythology.

The first known recorded Greek stories about the creation of heaven and earth occur in the 8th century BCE and were written by Hesiodos. Greek myths and sagas were collected and passed down by Homer, who lived in the 8th or 9th century B.C. His best-known works are the *Iliad* and the *Odyssey*. These are based on the story of the Trojan War. Greek myths dominate virtually all ancient literature. Even today, we see elements of Greek mythology in many classical musical works from the Middle Ages onward, in plays, visual art and literary works.

There are also modern stories about Greek mythology. It is still a popular theme now after thousands of years.

The creation of the world in Greek mythology

The most famous story about the creation of the world was Hesiodos' Theogonia.

In it play a role: Gaia, Tartaros, Eros, Pontus, Ouranos, the Titans (including Okeanos, Prometheus, Iapetus, Kronos, Hyperion, Tethys, Themis, Rhea and Theia), the Cyclopes, the Giants, the Erinyes, Hera, Hestia, Demeter, Hades, Poseidon, Zeus, Olympus, Aphrodite, Artemis, Pallas Athene, Apollo, Hephaestus, Typhon, the Moirs and Heracles.

Myths and sagas from Greek mythology

- The saga of Heracles, including the stories about the Giants, Eurystheus, the Hydra, the Centaurs, the Augias stable, the girdle of the Queen of the Amazons, the cattle of Geryones, the apple of the Hesperides, Kerberos (the guardian of the underworld) and the Centaur Nessus.
- The Argonauts, including the stories about Jason and the Golden Fleece.
- Theseus, with tales of the voyages to Athens and Crete, the battle of the Lapiths and Centaurs and Phaedra.
- Oedipus and the Labdacids, including stories about the Oracle of Delphi, the city of Colonus, the revenge quest of Polynices, Antigone in Thebes, Antigone and Creon.
- The Trojan War, including stories about Troy, Achilles' resentment, Apollo's revenge, the battle for Helena, and Andromache, Patroklos, Hector, Priamos, Penthesilea, Aiax, Menelaus, the horse of Troy, Laocoön and Sinon.
- The fate of the Tantalids, including tales of Atreus, Agamemnon, Orestes, the Erinyes, the Areopagus and Iphigenia in Tauris.
- The wanderings of Odysseus, including tales of Ithaca, Telemachos, the shipwreck, Nausikaä, the Phaeacians, the Lotophages, the Cyclopes, Polyphemus, Aeolus, the Laistrygonen, the phantom kingdom, the Sirens, Scylla and Charybdis, Helios, Eumaeus, Penelope, Circe, Laërtes and Hermes.

Immortals - Major Gods and Goddesses

Aphrodite

The goddess of love, beauty, and fertility

The Romans identified Aphrodite with their goddess
Venus.

In Greek mythology, **Aphrodite** (Ancient Greek: Ἀφροδίτη, *Aphrodítē*) is
the goddess of love, beauty, sexuality and fertility, among other things.
Some also consider her the goddess of balance. She originated from the
Phoenician goddess Astarte, but was so reformed by the Greeks
according to their disposition and needs that she became a truly Greek
goddess. She is often depicted with the god Eros and a goose.

Origin

Although the image of Aphrodite - mainly that of Aphrodite *Urania* - shows
many oriental features, her possibly oriental origins are controversial.
Some scholars ascribe to her an Indo-European origin, albeit with
decidedly oriental features. The role of Cyprus seems to have been
important for the oriental element in the Greek Aphrodite image. Beyond

the oriental hypothesis, there is Tümpel's unlikely contention that she would be of Thessalian origin, since her cult was very widespread in Thessaly and Boeotia. If in the naked woman whose genitals are strongly marked and who is surrounded by birds on some gold plates from Mycenaean shaft tombs we may already see a representation of Aphrodite, one must wonder to what extent also the Mycenaean and even the Minoan civilization was already under oriental influence. By some ancient authors she was considered the oldest of the Moirs (arranging goddesses).

The name of the month of April (lat. *aprīlis mēnsis*, from Etruscan *Apru*, derived from Greek *Aphrō*) comes from Aphrodite. The ancient calendar of Romulus called it the month of Venus.

Birth

There are several stories concerning Aphrodite's birth in Greek mythology or what may be counted as such. According to Homer, she was a daughter of Zeus and Dione, a titanid or oceanid. With this mother, the symbol of nature's fertility, returning the seed scattered in her with rich harvest, Aphrodite was sometimes identified, although Theia (Dione) as a separate divine being had her own meaning and personality.

Others call Aphrodite a daughter of Uranus and of the goddess of the day Hemera; still others try to reconcile the myths that differ about her origin by adopting three or four goddesses of that name.

The most famous, however, is the myth narrated by Hesiod, according to which Aphrodite arose from the silver foam (Greek: ἀφρός / aphrós) of the sea at the moment when the waves of the sea were fertilized by some falling drops of blood from the first world ruler and king of the gods, Uranus, after the latter had been castrated by his son Kronos with a diamond sickle and then deprived of dominion. She arose from the bars of the sea as the most beautiful of all women, white as the foam from which she was born, and loveliness and loveliness lay upon her smiling countenance and over all her being. Thus she was given the name Aphrodite, "the one born of foam," or *Anadyomene*, "the emerging one."

First she floated across the waters to the island of Kythira, whence she acquired the nickname (epiklese) "of Kythera," or *Kythereia*. Then she went to the island of Cyprus. Where she appeared, the desolate ground turned into blooming fields: flowers sprouted under her charming feet and the whole earth rejoiced in heavenly delight. A gentle breath of the Zephyr had carried her to the land. There the Horns of Spring awaited her to carry her to the immortal gods, or, as the famous sculptor Phidias depicted it, when she emerged from the sea, she was received by Eros (who then can hardly be considered her son, unless here there would be agreement with the older Egyptian myth of Isis, Osiris and Horus), wreathed by Peitho and soon surrounded by all the gods of heaven and earth.

Honors and epikleses

Aphrodite thus stands in relation to the three parts of the universe through her birth and descent. Her origin is in heaven, she was born of the sea, and the earth received her with all the splendor and glory that spring can give. This threefold relationship in which Aphrodite stands to nature had a great influence on her worship.

Indeed, she is first worshipped as *Urania*, this is the "Heavenly One," as the goddess who belongs to the heavenly gods and has her dwelling place with them.

Second, as *Aphrodite Pandemos*, this is that goddess who asserts her power over the whole land and the whole people. People have very often made the - erroneous - contrast between *Aphrodite Urania* as the goddess of pure, chaste love and *Aphrodite Pandemos* as that of sensual love. However, this view was not originally prevalent among the Greeks. The original conception of both these names was that *Aphrodite Urania* was a powerful goddess of the sky, the ancient goddess of nature, the symbol of nature's fertility, while *Aphrodite Pandemos*, on the other hand, was the goddess who, through her power - the need for love innate in every human being - pervades the entire nation.

A third Aphrodite, called *Euploia*, was a goddess of the sea and navigation. In these three capacities she was worshipped, for example, on the promontory of Cnidus in Asia Minor in three separate sanctuaries.

In other places the goddess was venerated for her extraordinary influence on the hearts of men, in whom she inspired love or aversion, and this *Aphrodite Epistrophia* or *Apostrophia*, reflected in the Roman *Venus Verticordia* that is "who turns the hearts," appeared as the third goddess in company with the *Aphrodite Urania* and *Pandemos*. However, later mythology made such a distinction between the various main forms in which the goddess was worshipped that even for each form a different genealogy was adopted.

Aphrodite Urania

Most segregated and distinct from the other forms of her worship was certainly that of *Aphrodite Urania*. It was the same worship service as that of *Aphrodite Akraia*, that is "on the heights," which was especially indigenous in Cyprus, at Cnidus, at Corinth and on Mount Eryx in Sicily. This service was very simple. No bloody sacrifices were allowed on her altars. The image of *Aphrodite Urania* was armed and she was worshiped together with Ares. Women were excluded from her worship almost everywhere. In Sicyon, where her priestesses had to observe strict chastity, she wore on her head a symbol of the celestial vault and in her hands a poppy and an apple, the symbols of fertility. Always *Aphrodite Urania* was represented as fully clothed, and people tried to give her images the stamp of seriousness and chastity, so that later she naturally became the symbol of pure love and marital fidelity. But her real significance as a goddess of nature was that of the starry sky, which brings down blessing and fertility from above, especially through the dew of cool nights. For example, it was believed on Mount Eryx that the great altar that the goddess possessed there was full of dew every morning and fresh grass that had grown during the night.

The actual symbol of this goddess was the moon, and in addition to the moon, she was also associated with the Venus star (the Greek Aphrodite was later identified with the Roman Venus).

This *Aphrodite Urania* was praised and invoked by the sages, and praised for her brightness, which she spread over the heavens by her great power, and the fertility, which she caused to descend from heaven to the earth.

Aphrodite Pandemos

More extensive, and more attractive to the greater part of the Greek people, was the worship of that Aphrodite who was not an abstract goddess of nature, but who asserted her power and her influence over the whole land and the whole people, that of *Aphrodite Pandemos*. This is the goddess of gardens and flowers, the charming goddess of spring, the goddess who charms the senses through love. She was especially associated with the beautiful flowers she produces, such as myrtles and roses. She revealed herself preferably in the fertile moisture of spring. When the Zephyr began to blow again and Zeus and Hera celebrated their wedding feast, when the heavens brought down fertilizing rain on the earth and the death sleep of winter gave way to the young, fresh life of spring, then was the time to worship *Aphrodite Pandemos*.

Greek poets liked to sing of her power, the power of love, as it reveals itself in all nature especially in spring. In that season, the goddess herself also tastes the sweet pleasure of love. She stays with Adonis on Cyprus, with Hephaistos on Limnos, with Ares at Thebes, with Anchises in the forests of the Ida Mountains. Obviously, the main festivals of this Aphrodite were celebrated in the spring, especially at Paphos and at Amathus in Cyprus, where the birth of Aphrodite from the sea was also celebrated.

Against the gaiety and exuberance of those spring festivals, however, there was also the deep, equally excessive sorrow, which characterized part of Aphrodite's worship at those festivals, which related to the death of Adonis.

This beautiful youth, who either grazed the flocks in the mountains as a shepherd or roamed the forests as a hunter was allowed to rejoice in the love of Aphrodite, until a wild boar killed him. The goddess searched for him, finally found his corpse and could not divorce him even from that corpse. At last the gods took pity on her and allowed Adonis to spend only half the year in the underworld, but during the other half he was allowed to enjoy the glorious light of the sun in the company of Aphrodite for as long as spring and summer lasted.

Especially in the East, very large festivals were attached to this myth. The disappearance of Adonis was then symbolically represented; people searched for him until they finally found his corpse and lamented him. All the ceremonies, all the lamentations, with which a burial ceremony was accompanied, were also performed and sung by the processionists, who carried away his image as that of a dead person, until at the end of the feast the joyful cry resounded: "*Adonis is alive and has risen!* ". Thus the news of his return turned sorrow into joy. People also maintained small gardens with short blooming flowers in his honor.

These feasts were an allusive representation of the ephemeral of the glories bestowed by spring, expressing the feeling of fear and gloom that besets man when everything in nature seems to be entering death sleep.

The myth tells of two children whom the goddess is said to have given to Adonis and mentions their names: Golgos and Beroë.

Aphrodite Euploia

13

Third, Aphrodite stands in relation to the sea. She is therefore called *Euploia*, that is *who bestows good sailing*. Other epithets indicating her connection with the sea are *Pontia (kai Liménia)* (*of the deep sea (and harbor)*), *Thalassía* (*of the sea*), *Liménia* (*of the harbor*), *Aligéna* (*sea-born*), *Epipóntia* (*from the sea*) and *Pelágia* (*of the coasts*). Of course, she was worshipped most often on the coasts in this capacity. She is a goddess of the calm, tranquil sea. She knows how to calm Poseidon, when he wants to create storms, and provides sailors with happy sailing and leads them into a safe harbor.

Other appearances of Aphrodite

These three representations of Aphrodite were joined by others. First, she was venerated as the goddess of beauty. She herself possessed such beauty, and every attraction a woman can have was completely hers. Her task was to bring out this beauty by adorning the body.

Acts of war, which express a masculine spirit, are entirely foreign to her. If she ventures into war, she suffers badly, as when she was wounded before Troy by Diomedes, who had the support of Pallas Athena. On the battlefield she cannot assert her power, and yet she is powerful. Not only does she help the Trojans endure the long battle by the support, which she lends to her darling Paris and her son Aeneas, but she subdues all whom she wishes to bring under her power by the irresistible power of her beauty.

The golden Aphrodite, the sweetly smiling Aphrodite, are epithets referring to this attribute. She wears the girdle of love, which contains within her all the magics that love has at its disposal: the fierce desire and the sweet language of love, which cause even the minds of the sensible to stray from the straight path. Her eyes, her beautiful bosom, her lovely mouth, which is compared to a rosebud, are often sung with enthusiasm by the Greek poets. When one wants to emphasize the exquisite beauty of a mortal woman, one compares her to Aphrodite.

By the Horns and the Charites she has herself wreathed with spring flowers; her clothes are permeated with the scents of these flowers. This simple yet beautiful decoration of the goddess with flowers was also adopted by the visual arts, which tried to represent in Aphrodite the ideal of feminine beauty. In the East this was deviated from, in genuine Ancient Greek art it was not.

In addition to the epithets already mentioned, the goddess was worshiped under several other names, especially after the places, where she had temples, such as *Kypris, Kythereia, Kytherea* (after the island of Cyprus), *Paphia* (after the city of Paphos), *Amathusia* (after the city of Amathus), *Idalia* (after Mount Ida), *Knidia* (after the city of Cnidus), *Erykine/Erykina* (after the temple dedicated to Aphrodite on Mount Eryx in Sicily) or *Akadalia* (named after the spring of the same name in Boeotia, where Aphrodite bathed with the Charites).

Among her other nicknames deserve mention:

- *Areia*, that is "the warrior," alluding to the intimate bond by which she was connected to Ares. As a result, to some extent she herself had become a goddess of war. Especially in Sparta, where women excelled in extraordinary beauty, she was venerated under that name. There she had a temple with a very ancient statue bearing arms. Later, the service of *Aphrodite Areia* was also transferred to Corinth, Kythera and Cyprus.
- *Aphrodite Anadyomene*, means "rising from the sea" and refers to the birth of Aphrodite from the foam of the surging sea.
- *Aphrodite Erykine* was a nickname of Aphrodite after Mount Eryx in Sicily, where she had a magnificent temple on the northwestern tip. This temple, it was said, had been founded by her son Eryx, whom she had given birth to from Butes. By the same name the goddess was worshiped at Psophis in Arcadia, where Psophis, the daughter of Eryx, built her a temple. The service of this goddess was spread throughout Sicily and came from there at the beginning of the Second Punic War to Rome, where a temple was erected to her in the year 217 B.C. after the Battle of Lake Trasimeno. A second temple was built in front of the *Porta Collina* in 181 BCE.
- *Aphrodite Hetaira* was originally a goddess who protected and controlled the intimate bond of friendship; later she became the patron goddess of those women in Athens who, as we have seen above, devoted their lives entirely to the service of this goddess and dared to compare themselves with her.
- *Aphrodite Kallipygos*, who was especially venerated in Sicily, was referred to by this nickname as "the goddess with the clean buttocks." This eccentric nickname was explained by a legend, native to Syracuse. There, two sisters got into a fight which of them surpassed the other in beauty as far as this part of the body was concerned. They called in a young man as arbiter, who decided in favor of the older sister and was so captivated by her beauty that he wanted to make her his wife. He communicated the

matter to his younger brother, who now conceived love for the younger sister, and although the girls were daughters of a simple farmer and the boys sons of a wealthy citizen of Syracuse, the latter consented to his sons marrying the farmer's daughters. In gratitude for this, the two sisters erected a temple at Syracuse in honor of *Aphrodite Kallipygos*, in which the statue of the goddess was placed with her robe suspended above the hips.

- *Aphrodite Ktesylla* was the name of the goddess who stood in a temple at Iulis on the island of Kea. After Hermochares buried his wife Ktesylla, whom he had lost when she bore him a son, a dove flew up to heaven from the coffin. Her corpse had disappeared. The oracle of Delphi thereupon declared, that Aphrodite had taken her to herself and that in her memory a temple should be built to *Aphrodite Ktesylla*.
- At Sparta, at the same time as an *Aphrodite Urania*, whose image was represented armed, an *Aphrodite Morpho* was also worshiped, apparently a goddess of chaste love and marital fidelity.
- *Aphrodite Melainis* ("the black one"), also called *Aphrodite Melaina*, seems to have had special worship in Thespiae, in Melangeia and in Corinth. This epiklese of Aphrodite seems to have indicated the chtonic nature of Aphrodite, as a goddess of fertility.
- *Aphrodite Nymphia* was the protector of the betrothed and the newlyweds, who was given her own sanctuary just outside Troezen by Theseus when the latter took Helena to wife. Her nickname was derived from νύμφη / nýmphê, a term for a girl passing from adolescence to married woman.
- *Aphrodite Peitho* was an amalgamation of Aphrodite with her companion Peitho, emphasizing the aspect of marriage and betrothal, which was already patronized by both deities and was now even more closely linked to Aphrodite, as it were, through the fusion of the two goddesses.
- *Aphrodite Xene*, that is "the strange Aphrodite," was the name under which it was claimed that Menelaus had erected a temple to Aphrodite in Egypt. Indeed, when Paris, after having shaken Helena, went to Troy, he also entered Egypt, but the king of that country, Proteus, kept her for himself and chased Paris out of the country, either alone or with a false image of her. Helena, however, he kept with him, and he later returned her with the treasures looted by Paris to Menelaus, who in gratitude erected a temple to Aphrodite. The Romans called this goddess *Venus Hospita*.

- The so-called *Aphrodite of Aphrodisias*, the city goddess of Aphrodisias in Anatolia, appears to have been an original Carian deity who would fuse into a trinity of Aphrodite *Ourania*, *Pandemos* and *Pelagia*. In this capacity, Aphrodite was worshiped throughout the Mediterranean until the Roman imperial period. Emperor Hadrian, among others, was an ardent worshipper of her. In the 5th century, however, her temple was converted into a Christian basilica. Today, the statue stands in Paris, where it is still visited daily by tourists.
- *Isis-Aphrodite* was the association made of her in Egypt. Representations in polychromed terracotta of the naked goddess, crowned by a cornucopia transformed into a basket or cornucopia, were commonly given to young couples as wedding gifts, expressing the desire for fertility. After death, these were given as grave gifts. The association with Egypt is explained by the Greeks' great admiration for the antiquity of this culture. The well-to-do even went to study there partly for this reason.

Aphrodites parties

The *Aphrodisia* were festivals celebrated in honor of Aphrodite, mainly on the island of Cyprus, and most commonly in the city of Paphos. During these festivals, no bloody sacrifices were allowed to be made to the goddess, who was worshipped here under the guise of a pointed round cone or of a small white pyramid. The flame of the sacrificial fire, frankincense and myrrh were pleasing to her. Later, the *Aphrodisia* seem to have been accompanied by mysteries dedicated to Aphrodite. *Aphrodisia* were also celebrated at the temple of Aphrodite at Amathus, which after that of Paphos was the most famous temple of the goddess in Cyprus, as well as on the island dedicated to her, Kythera. Furthermore, *Aphrodisia* were celebrated at Aigina, at Thebes, at Corinth and at Athens, although they were most likely known throughout Greece. In most places the hetaires participated in these festivals with their lovers.

At the temple on the Eryx in Sicily, curious festivals were celebrated: the *Anagogia* and *Katagogia*. In and near that temple, in fact, numerous doves were kept, which at a certain time all flew away, it was said, to Libya. This was considered the departure of Aphrodite and celebrated with a feast, the *Anagogia*. Nine days later, the doves returned with a strange, extraordinarily beautiful dove in front. This was called the return of the goddess, which was festively celebrated by the *Katagogia*.

Aphrodite in relation to other gods and mortals

As mentioned, Aphrodite is a goddess of love and fertility. She bestows upon mortals the captivating charm that engenders love, but she also instills the consuming passion of love. She herself preceded with her example. She has felt the passion of love, she has made more than one happy by giving him her love. She married Hephaistos, the crippled god of fire, but the latter was not long allowed to rejoice in her loyalty. The masculine, warlike Ares, the god of war managed to win her over. When Hephaistos noticed his wife's adultery with Ares, he crafted an artful net. While both lovers thought themselves safe from any disturbance, they were suddenly caught in that net by Hephaistos and abandoned to the mocking glances and words of the other gods.

From that union of Aphrodite and Ares sprang seven children: Harmonia, Deimos, Phobos, Eros, Himeros, Pothos and Anteros.

Aphrodite was also in a very close relationship to Hermes. The fruit of their union was Hermaphroditus.

With Dionysos, according to some, she was the mother of Priapos. With this god of fertility she seems to have a close relationship, as we find several sanctuaries of Aphrodite and Dionysos near each other.

But not only gods, even mortals were sometimes allowed to rejoice in the love of the goddess. We already saw this with Adonis. That the goddess did not appreciate people making fun of her amorous adventures is shown by the following legend: when the muse Clio made fun of Aphrodite's love for Adonis, she was punished by the goddess with love for Pieros, to whom she gave birth to Hyakinthos.

The myth goes on to tell of her love for the Trojan shepherd prince Anchises, whom she sought out in the shady forests of the Ida Mountains. She bore him a son Aeneas, whom throughout his life she always stood by as a faithful mother. She rescued him when he was wounded in battle, carried him with his father safely out of Troy, when the city was destroyed and almost all the unfortunate inhabitants perished. She stood by him in all the difficulties he had to encounter on his wanderings, and through her efforts it was given to him to lay the foundations of the Roman empire, which would one day dominate the world. Her affection was transferred to his descendants, who called themselves after Ascanius, the son of Aeneas Julii, so that even the great reformer of the Roman state, Julius Caesar, thought he could rejoice in Aphrodite's special favor.

Also Butes, one of the Argonauts, who, lured by the song of the Sirens, jumped from the Argo into the sea, was allowed to share in the love of Aphrodite, by whom he was saved and cherished. She bore him a son named Eryx.

Others, if not in love, were allowed to rejoice in the outstanding favor of the goddess. Among these should be mentioned in the first place Paris, the son of the Trojan king Priamus. Indeed, Aphrodite was indebted to him. For when the goddess of strife, Eris, at the wedding feast of Peleus and Thetis, to which she alone of all the gods and goddesses had not been invited, had thrown a golden apple with the inscription "to the most beautiful," and Hera, Athena and Aphrodite disputed each other's possession of it, Paris was appointed arbitrator by Zeus. He assigned the apple to Aphrodite, guided to do so by the goddess's irresistible beauty and by the promise she made to him, that she would grant him the love of the most beautiful woman on earth. She fulfilled this promise by winning him the heart of Helena, wife of the Spartan king Menelaus. Always Aphrodite continued to protect and favor Paris, until he fell by the sword of the Greeks shortly before or at the fall of Troy.

Hippomenes, the son of Meleager, also enjoyed the goddess' affection when he raced Atalante. The latter lived alone in the forests and challenged anyone who desired her hand to a race. He then had to start the run unarmed toward a certain goal. She followed him with a lance and pierced him, when she had caught up with him and thus conquered him. However, Aphrodite gave Hippomenes three beautiful golden apples, which he threw at Atalante's feet one by one during the run. Surprised by the sight of these magnificent trinkets, the Atalante, who was running after him, stooped down to pick them up one by one. But she lost so much time as a result, that the lucky lover reached the goal first.

In another version of the story it is narrated, that Atalante's heart remained cold even for the love of Meleager, but that afterwards Meilainion, the son of Amphidamas, captivated by her beauty, when she fled from him too, pursued her incessantly and suffered and fought for her. He served her without growing tired, until at last Aphrodite endeared her heart and she married Meilainion.

In Cyprus, people knew of Cinyras, the first priest of the goddess, the creator of the lamentations sung at the festivals (*Adonia*) commemorating the death of Adonis. To him was attributed the institution of the nocturnal festivals celebrated in honor of the goddess (*pervigilia Veneris*). The goddess bestowed on him beauty, wealth, ability, happiness, all that he retained until old age, and after his death his ashes and later those of his descendants were allowed to rest in her temple.

Furthermore, Pygmalion was rewarded for his faithful adherence to the goddess's service, in that she gave breath and life to an ivory statue made by him, which bore the name of Galathea, for which he was inflamed in love, that it might become to him a companion of life.

When a certain Selemnos, who had been deserted by his beloved, the spring nymph Argyra, when his beauty diminished, was consumed by grief because of this, Aphrodite, who took pity on him, turned him into a river, which possessed this property that whoever bathed in it was henceforth tormented by the grief of love.

As the goddess of love, Aphrodite engenders this passion in the minds of men. Especially in the hearts of women, she ignites it like a consuming fire. We already saw an example of this in Helena, to whom she instilled a love for Paris so great that she was tempted to leave husband, child and homeland.

Similarly, she managed to ignite in Medea such a fierce passion for Iason, that she forgot all sense of duty and love for her parents, to follow the beloved man.

Aphrodite it was also, who blinded the hearts of Pasiphaë and of Ariadne by passion and who made Phaedra conceive an unholy love for her stepson Hippolytus, who had devoted himself to the service of Artemis. Hence a struggle between the two goddesses, which ended in the sad death of their protégés.

For Psyche, too, Aphrodite had a similar fate in mind, when she commanded her son Eros to take one of his sharpest golden arrows, to pierce Psyche's heart with it, that she might awaken in her breast an incurable love for the meanest and least of all men who dwelt on the earth. But when Eros injured himself by his arrow, he himself was overcome with love for Psyche and decided to keep her love to himself. Eventually he managed to reconcile his mother and the lovers were able to stay together.

When the Propoitides, girls from Amathus in Cyprus denied that Aphrodite was a goddess, to punishment for this, they became the first to be beset with such a need for sensual love that they sank to the deepest level of humiliation. Then they were turned into stones by the goddess out of pity.

20

Aphrodite would also raise Klytia and Kameiro, daughters of Pandareos and Harmothea, after their parents died because of their participation in the atrocities of Tantalos.

That power of Aphrodite, which she can exercise through the passion of love, is an inexhaustible material for the Greek poets, for that power is infinite. It extends even over the realm of the dead. Those made unhappy by love on earth still wander restlessly in a separate place in the underworld.

Aphrodite also bestows the pleasure of love. To savor that is even a duty to her. Whoever disdains or despises it is her enemy. Since Hippolytos despised the love offered to him by Phaidra, she caused his death. Since Narcissus remained insensitive to the love of the beautiful nymph Echo, she instilled in him a love for himself, which became the cause of his death.

This trait in the goddess' being gave rise to an institution that seems strange to us. Attached to many of her temples were priestesses, who observed the temple service, performed music and dances at her festivals, but would also give themselves at some point to anyone who desired them (Hierodules). However, there is much ambiguity about these institutions and recent research has questioned this so-called temple prostitution of the hierodules.

In ancient times, this was seen as a regulatory institution, so Solon prescribed these institutions in his laws. Among some, *Aphrodite Pandemos*, who was worshipped in such a way, because of this institution, was no longer held in high regard, because they had a different view of sexuality.

Aphrodite was also the goddess of "pure" sensual love. Love, which is the maker of the reproduction of the human race, without which no state can continue to exist, even when purified by the sacred institution of marriage, was a corollary of her being. The most beautiful thing Aphrodite can bestow upon a girl is a happy marriage. This is the pinnacle of happiness that the woman receives from her hand. Under her protection was the female youth and she was also close to the married woman in the difficult hours, when she gave birth to her children. Hence, she was often invoked with Artemis and the separate goddess Eileithyia, who in later times was of particular help to women giving birth, represented as much a part of her being as of that of Artemis.

Pure, faithful, conjugal love, domestic discipline and honor, that was what she took under her wing. But all that was attributed to *Aphrodite Urania*, and hence the strong contrast, which, although not situated in the original essence of the goddess, was made in later times by some between the *Urania* and the *Pandemos*.

At the end of the classical period, the affluence of certain *poleis* made the service of Aphrodite more magnificent, to which the "hetaeren," companion ladies who often stayed in the company of the most distinguished men, also contributed. These were beautiful, often sagacious, witty and developed. Hetaeren often allowed themselves to be compared to Aphrodite, or depicted as Aphrodite by sculptors or painters.

Aphrodites companions

Aphrodite was always surrounded by a multitude of beings whose main task was to add to her beauty and grace. First of all, the Horns and Charites were always in her company. We have already seen that it is they who clothe and embellish her and adorn her with the belt, in which dwells the magic of love, which gives the goddess her power over gods and men. Further Peitho, the goddess of flattering persuasion, Eros, Pothos and Hymenaeus, i. e. "the god of love," "desire" and "fierce desire," and finally the Hymen or Hymenaios, the god of marriage and the wedding feast.

Aphrodites attributes

To Aphrodite was sanctified everything distinguished by extraordinary fertility: thus in the plant kingdom the myrtle and the apple (μῆλον / mēlon: ooft), among the animals the ram, the buck, the hare, the dove, the sparrow and the dolphins. The swan was also traditionally called a favorite bird of the goddess, but the mirror should also be mentioned, which the goddess is said to have used when Paris passed his judgment on the Ida, while Hera and Athena failed to do so.

Aphrodite in the visual arts

Now as for the statues of Aphrodite, they were found in large numbers all over Greece in ancient times.

However, one must distinguish between the oldest symbolic representations of the goddess and the images, which owed their origin to the later, developed Greek art. For example, at Paphos in Cyprus she was worshiped in the form of a cone or pyramid placed in the most sacred part of the temple (*naos*). Among the images of Aphrodite proper, a great distinction could be observed in the representation of *Aphrodite Urania* and the images of that Aphrodite, who also remained near and accompanied the short, transient earthly beauty which she had bestowed until the grave (*Aphrodite Epitumbidia*), and the representation of the goddess of sensual love, beauty, charm and pleasure. The former carries as attributes a dove, an apple, a flower or an egg and is usually covered with clothing; the latter, on the other hand, is usually completely or partially naked, carries a buck or a hare and often carries a mirror in her hand. Among the most famous statues of the goddess in antiquity was that in her temple at Cnidus, made by the Athenian sculptor Praxiteles.

This artist was the creator of the ideal that the Greek artists tried to achieve in their representations of Aphrodite. Also, an Aphrodite decorated with clothes on the island of Kos by the same artist seems to have been among the most outstanding works of art of antiquity.

Another famous image of Aphrodite, together with Eros and Pan is also attributed to Praxiteles. From this image one can see that the sandal had an erotic connotation in Greek culture. Similarly, sandals of hetairen have been found with the message "follow me."

 Several famous paintings by Greek masters also depicted the goddess.

Among these, the *Aphrodite Anadyomene* of Apelles was the most famous. As such a charming foam goddess emerging from the flood, she was depicted in the painting considered the masterpiece of the great Greek painter Apelles. She was completely naked and depicted drying her hair with her hands. The inhabitants of the island of Kos hung this painting in the temple of Asklepios; Emperor Augustus later took it to Rome and, as compensation, waived part of the taxes that the inhabitants of Kos had to raise. He had it hung in the temple of Divus Julius (the deified Julius Caesar). Already by the time of Emperor Nero, the painting had been completely obliterated and had to be replaced by another work of art.

Of the surviving statues of Aphrodite, the most beautiful and renowned is the so-called Venus of Milo found on the island of Melos (now Milo) in the year 1820. As the image shows, in this statue the upper part of the body is naked and the lower limbs are covered from the hips down with a thin robe. Since the arms are lost, it cannot be determined with certainty, what image the artist had in mind when making this statue.

After these, the first thing to be mentioned is the so-called "Medici Venus," now in Florence. This statue was found in Rome. On the pedestal, an Athenian artist named Kleomenes is named as the maker. The time in which this artist lived is entirely uncertain. Probably the statue is no older than the time of Emperor Augustus.

Another famous statue is the so-called "Vénus accroupie." The goddess is depicted at the moment she is stooping down in the bathtub. This statue is counted among the most beautiful and lovely representations that have survived of Aphrodite.

One of the most copied images is probably the "Aphrodite of Fréjus" or so-called "Venus Genetrix." Here the goddess is represented more as a maternal goddess. She is covered with an undergarment that closes around the body, leaving only the left breast exposed. With a graceful movement of the right arm she is just pulling up her upper garment of coarser fabric that falls backwards. The face is rounder than in those sculptures modelled on Praxiteles; the expression of chaste morality and feminine dignity that the sculptor has managed to give it, make a striking impression.

Finally, mention should be made of a statue of Aphrodite found near the theater of Arles, ancient Arelate, the so-called Venus of Arles, now in the museum of the Louvre in Paris.

As already mentioned, one can recognize in Aphrodite more clearly than in any other Greek deity the oriental origin. The goddess who in the various Eastern religions was similar in essence and nature to the Greek Aphrodite, bore different names in different regions, of which we mention here Mylitta, Alilat and Astarte.

By the Romans, she was identified with their Venus.

Trivia

According to a single tradition, Helena, mother of Constantine the Great, found the true cross of Christ hidden in a crypt under Aphrodite's temple in Jerusalem in the 4th century.

A bronze statue of Aphrodite was found in the Tapsiris Magna temple in May 2008, along with a decapitated statue of a king from the Ptolemaic dynasty that ruled Egypt from 323 to 30 B.C. The find was made near

Alexandria by a collaborating team of archaeologists from Egypt and the Dominican Republic searching for Cleopatra's tomb.

Apollo

The god of light, youth, beauty, poetry, and music

Made one of the chief gods of Rome by the emperor Augustus. Apollo was considered primarily a god of healing by the Romans, who began worshipping him during an epidemic in about 431 bc. He was later made one of the chief gods of Rome by the emperor Augustus. The emperor regarded him as his patron deity and had a magnificent temple built in his honor.

Apollo (Ancient Greek: Ἀπόλλων, *Apóllōn*) was one of the most important deities of Greek mythology. Of all the gods, his worship was the most widespread among the Greek people and enjoyed the highest esteem. Under the Latinized name Apollo, he became known in Rome.

By the Greek poets, he is usually called **Phoibos Apollo**. Apollo is also considered the representative of rational beauty and order, as opposed to Dionysos, who symbolizes emotional intoxication.

Etymology

The etymology of the name "Apollo" is uncertain. Among ancient authors, however, we find several folk etymologies. Thus, Plato in his *Cratylus* relates the name to ἀπόλυσις / apólysis, "liberation," to ἀπόλουσις / apólousis, "the wiping; cleansing," with ἀπλοῦν / haploūn, "simple," referring in particular to the Thessalian form of his name, Ἄπλουν / Áploun, and finally with Ἀει-βάλλων / Aei-bállôn, "the always striking one." Plutarchus in his Moralia (*The E of Delphi*; 354 f) also mentions ἀπλοῦν / haploūn, in the sense of "singular."

Origin

While in the 19th century it was still thought that Apollo was the god of light, who found his highest development in the sun, today people think differently.

Although he became the most Greek of the gods, Apollo seems to have come to Greece relatively late. He was possibly brought to Greece at the end of the Mycenaean civilization (ca. 1200-1100 BCE) by the invading Dorians, although it is also possible that he came from Hittite Asia Minor. It is now believed that its origins were in central Anatolia (see Hyperborea). One clue is that the Homeric hymn to Apollo recounts how the god came over Delos to Delphi. His epithet *Hekatos* (far striking) can be related to the Carian Hekate. On Hittite cuneiform tablets (the so-called treaty of Alaksandu between the Hittites and Wilusa, which is sometimes identified with Troy) the name *Appaliunas* or *Apalunas appears*, probably closely related to Apollo.

He seems to have originally been a god of flocks (Apollo *Karneios* and *Smintheus*), who was the patron not only of shepherds (*Apollo Agreus* and *Nomios*), but also of their enemy, the wolf (*Apollo Lykeios*). His protection of archery (*Apollo Hekatos*), medicine (*Apollo Paian*) and music (*Apollo Musagetes*) was probably related to his function as a shepherd god.

Birth

Apollo is the son of Zeus and Leto and the twin brother of Artemis. When Leto was pregnant, she was pursued for a long time by Hera, the jealous wife of Apollo's sire Zeus. She could find no refuge to quietly await the birth of her children except on the island of Delos where Apollo and Artemis were born.

Nicknames and functions

Because of his extensive and wide-ranging work, many names and epikleses have arisen for Apollo.

Apollo Karneios

Apollo *Karneios* (an Ancient Greek word for *ram*) is considered the god of flocks of sheep among the Dorian tribes. According to legend, once the Dorians, led by the Heraclids from Naupaktos, were about to cross to the Peloponnese when Hippotes, one of the Heraclids, killed the seer Karnos, who was a lover of Apollo. After that, plague had come over the army. The disease disappeared only after Hippotes was driven out and Apollo's anger was atoned for by the institution of a feast. The Spartans celebrated this feast, called the Karneia, in memory of the help the god had rendered them by leading them to the Peloponnese.

Apollo Smintheus

Apollo himself had cattle, which grazed in Pieria at the foot of Olympos. The fields and field fruits were also under Apollo's protection.

Apollo Agreus

Apollo was also much into hunting, usually together with his sister Artemis. From the horns of wild goats, which Artemis had killed on Kynthos, he built his first altar. As a hunter, Apollo was nicknamed *Agreus*.

Apollo Nomios

As a shepherd, Apollo was nicknamed *Nomios*. He is said to have served as a shepherd with Laomedon and with Admetos.

Apollo Lykios

Apollo, under the nickname *Lykios, was* also worshipped as a god of light and sun, not only in Greece, but especially on the coasts of Asia Minor. The Asia Minor landscape of Lycia was probably named after him.

Apollo Hekatos

As an archer, he was usually called *Hekatos*, *Hekatebolos* or *Hekabolos* (translating) or the one famous by his bow, or the god with the silver bow given to him by Hephaistos. Apollo's arrows never missed their mark. The overconfident who were thus punished included Niobe and her children, the army of the Greeks before Troy, the Cyclopes, Eurytos, Otus and Ephialtes and the Giants.

Apollo Pythios

Already shortly after his birth, Apollo killed with his arrows the mega-serpent Python, which was making the sanctuary of Pytho near Mount Parnassus unsafe. Because of this victory, Apollo was nicknamed *Pythios*, "the Pythian. He would make this shrine his own, which became known as the Oracle of Delphi. He was honored at the Pythian Games under this name.

God of prophecy

Apollo's most important attribute revealed itself in his gift of prophecy. At his birth, he had uttered the words "I will proclaim the undeviating will of Zeus." He also founded the famous temple at Delphi and took possession of the ancient oracle of Gaia (the Earth) there.

Apollo Archigetes

Because as a result of those rulings of the Delphic oracle very often the foundation of cities or the sending out of colonies was undertaken, he was also revered as Apollo *Archigetes* (leader of the colonists).

Thus Apollo is said to have helped Cretan or Arcadian settlers found the city of Troy, which explains his pro-Trojan stance in the *Iliad*. It is also said to have been Apollo himself, who led the Dorians on their journey through Greece to Kedaimon, Messene and other cities of the Peloponnese; numerous cities, scattered all over the world, considered him its very founder and named themselves after him Apollonia.

God of the clty

In the cities themselves, he paved the roads and streets. Hence his nickname *Aguieus*. In front of each residence was a quadrangular block of stone dedicated to him, and where the narrow width of the street did not permit such placement they painted it on the wall. As protector of the markets, he bore the nickname of *Agoraios*. With Laomedon he built the walls of Troy, with Alkathoös those of Megara.

Apollo Amyklaios

The worship of Apollo *Amyklaios* had its seat mainly in the Laconic city of Amyklai. It had already been in vogue among the first inhabitants of Laconia, then passed to the Achaeans and then to the Dorians.

This service was in connection with the death of Hyakinthos, in whose honor in the hottest summer time, in the dog days, the Hyakinthians were celebrated by the Spartans at Amyklai. Hyakinthos, a son of Amyklas, was a lover of Apollo, but he was accidentally killed by the latter when playing with the *discus* (throwing disc) (either by fate or by the spurned lover Zephyros). His tomb was located under the altar and statue of the god. The first day of the Hyakinthians was a mournful feast in memory of Hyakinthos' sad death, but the second day was a joyous feast commemorating how he had been taken to heaven by Apollo and had thus entered a new, a more glorious life through death.

Apollo Delphinios

Apollo *Delphinios* is the guide over the sea. Just as he as *Agyieus* (cf. *supra*) makes the streets and roads safe, so he as *Delphinios* paves the paths of the sea in spring, the beginning of the season of light. The dark clouds he breaks by the power of his light and he sends the dolphins as friendly companions to the mortals, who sail the sea, to proclaim their prosperity. On seacoasts he was highly revered; very many of the most beautiful temples of Apollo were located near the sea.

Phoibos Apollo

From about 410-400 B.C., the philosophical idea of Apollo as god of the sun who was referred to as *Phoibos arose*. He is also said to have derived this nickname from his grandmother Phoibe and to have had the meaning of "prophet." At the time of Homer, however, this function was reserved for the deity Helios who would later merge into Apollo under the name Apollo *Helios*. Nevertheless, Apollo and Helios remained separate deities in mythological texts.

Relationship with gods and humans

According to certain legends, Apollo maintained close ties with the Hyperboreans living in the far north. Such stories may have come from travelers who had visited the area in question. Myth has it that Apollo divided his time between the Hyperboreans, with whom he stayed in winter, and the Greeks, with whom he was in summer.

Amorous relationships and children

Apollo, as a handsome young god, had many love affairs with both nymphs and mortal women. Once he had conceived love for Daphne, the daughter of the river god Peneus, who, however, felt nothing for him. As she fled to escape his advances, she asked her father to change her appearance to get rid of him. And so it happened. The nymph changed into a laurel tree, which was henceforth dedicated to Apollo.

He fathered the *heros* Ion, progenitor of the Ionians, with Creüsa, daughter of the Attic king Erechtheus, whom he had seduced. The *heros* Asklepios was his son from his relationship with the Thessalian Koronis. He also founded the city of Cyrene after kidnapping the athletic nymph Cyrene, with whom he was in love, to that place in Libya where this city was to be founded. With her he would have a son named Aristaios.

In addition to his adventures with women, the god also maintained relationships with beautiful men, the most famous of which are those with Hyakinthos and Kyparissos. When they had died to Apollo's great sorrow, he turned the former into a flower (similar to our hyacinth), the latter into a tree, the cypress.

His least successful adventure was with the Trojan princess Cassandra, who had first agreed to share bed with him in exchange for the gift of foretelling the future, but as soon as Apollo granted her wish, she refused to keep her promise. Since Apollo could not undo a granted gift, he added to her gift, as punishment, the restriction that no one would believe her predictions.

In the visual arts

Apollo is usually represented as a youthful god, tall, strong and handsome, with majestic, tidy gaze and head covered with richly wavy, blond locks. Older art gave him the appearance of a man of mature age, with powerful physique and stern features, but beardless; later Greek art usually depicted him as a young man.

The most famous statue of Apollo, which has survived to our times, is the *Apollo of Belvedere*, excavated in 1503 near Antium on the coast of central Italy, today's Nettuno. It is uncertain whether the artist intended to depict the god with a bow in his left hand, or with the aigis and in its center the Medusa head.

Attributes

Of the trees, as we saw the laurel was sanctified to him above all; of the animals: the wolf, the doe, the swan, the dolphin, the raven, the crow and the snake (medicine). His ordinary attributes are bow and arrows, a laurel wreath, the zither and the lyre.

His main temples were those already mentioned at Delphi, on Delos, further at Amyclae and at Clarus near Colophon.

Ares

Ares was associated with the Roman god Mars.

Ares (Ancient Greek: Ἄρης, *Arês*; genitivus Ἄρεως, *Areôs*) is a figure from Greek mythology. He is the god of war and personification of warrior spirit. The Roman name for Ares is Mars.

Origin

The god Ares is the son of Zeus and Hera (Homer, *Iliad* V 890; Hesiodos, *Theogonia* 921f.). According to Homer, he is the fatal instigator of the bloody battle, a murderous warrior, who finds the highest pleasure in clanging weapons and wreaking carnage, plunges with joy into the enemy ranks, and cheers at the fall of the defeated, at the death cries of the dying and at the sight of the corpse-covered battlefield.

Yet Ares also embodies the virtues of warfare. Homer describes Meriones, for example, with the words "bold as Ares," "as brave as Ares" (*Iliad* XIII 295-330, transl. M.A. Schwartz) and "as Ares so swift" (*Iliad* XIII 529).

Nestor also refers to the Greek soldiers in a speech as "servants of Ares" (*Iliad* VI 50-85). The epithets Homer uses to describe Ares also indicate his martial ability. The most common is "man-killer," but in addition, "blood-stained" and "wall stormer" are also used (*Iliad* V 450-460).

It is also said that the wars are not created by Ares, but that Ares comes when they are already in progress. Although he loves the massacres, he respects the rules.

His birthplace and true home was thought to be at the edge of the Greek world, among the barbaric and warlike Thracians (*Iliad* XIII 301; Ovid). He therefore retreated to Thrace after being caught in bed with Aphrodite. The two lovers were caught in the bed in which they made love by a cunning trap: the bed that Hephaistos and his wife Aphrodite usually shared. The bed was thrown against the ceiling with a net of iron chains, made by Hephaistos, through which they were caught entangled in each other. In this way Hephaistos managed to make the adultery known (*Odyssey* VIII 303-304.). The disgrace caused Aphrodite and Ares to flee from Olympos. Ares left for Thrace, and Aphrodite for Paphos (*Odyssey* VIII 348-355.).

Although Ares' half-sister Athena is also a war deity, Athena is the goddess of strategic warfare while Ares is more the god of the unpredictable violence of war with all its possible outcomes.

Ares' worship and epikleses

In Tegea Ares was venerated under the epiklese "Gynaikothoinas," i. e. celebrated by women. This name he owed to the fact that Marpessa, when her city was greatly cornered by the Lakedaimonians, having armed all the women and girls, who were able to bear arms to come to the aid of the men, won a brilliant victory, for which the women instituted a feast in honor of Ares, which was to be celebrated only by women (Paus., VIII 48.4.).

In addition, he was also venerated under the name *Ares "Aphneios"*, i. e. the abundant one, on Mount Kresios, near Tegea, because there he allowed his son Aeropos whose mother Aerope had died at birth to still drink milk in abundance from the breast of his already deceased mother (Pope., VIII 44.7.). He also had further in Arcadia an altar at Megalopolis (Pope., VIII 32.3.) and at the sanctuary of Despoine near Akakesion (Pope., VIII 37.12.).

Under the name *Ares "Hippios,"* d. i. of horses, he was venerated together with *Athena Hippias* at Olympia, where the Elijans offered sacrifices once a month on all the altars present there (Pope., V 15.6.).

Along the road from Therapne to Sparta he had a sanctuary under the name *Ares "Theritas"* (Θηρίτας), of which Pausanias (III 19.7.) says that it was believed that this epithet was derived from the name of his nurse Thero - for which Pausanias sees a Kolkidian origin - but rather believed himself that it meant "brutal." Sam Wide suggests the contention that the name may well be of Boeotic origin. However, it is also possible that it is a pre-Doric cult since this oldest sanctuary to Ares was located in Laconia in the oldest city on the Greek mainland, Therapne.

In Athens the hill *Areios Pagos* (*Areopagus*) named after him and the court established there were sanctified to him. However, he himself had been the first to be called to account on this hill by the immortal gods, since he too had to submit to the established order and law. For Halirrhothios, the son of Poseidon, dishonored Alkippe, the daughter of Ares, who then attacked him and killed him. When Poseidon brought the murderer before the court of the gods, they acquitted him of all guilt.

On the whole, people in Greece paid less tribute to Ares than to other gods, although he had temples, altars and statues here and there. Only in Thebes and in Thrace, which was inhabited by savage tribes, was he not pushed into the background. The latter country was his favorite abode, because the gods of the rivers of this country, the Hebros, Tmolos and Strimon applied to his sons, and the bloody human sacrifices, which were offered to him there, seemed to correspond perfectly with the bloodthirsty character of the god of war, at least in the rougher times. In Scythia, where he was venerated under the symbol of a sword, they sacrificed to him horses and men, and every hundredth man of the captives.

Ares in relation to other gods and mortals

His ferocity made him hated even by the immortal gods, by his father Zeus and especially by Athena. More than once the latter wounded him in the battle before Troy, where she assisted the Greeks, he the Trojans. She also aimed the lance of Diomedes, who managed to wound the god with it. Then he screamed as loudly as 9000 or 10000 men together would scream.

He is conquered by Athena every time, because he fights out of wild lust to fight but without policy, order or regularity, while Athena does not deny the great giftedness of her mind even in battle. He cares neither for what is right or wrong, nor for the salvation of the vanquished, nor for the disasters of the vanquished.

Repeatedly Homer paints him thus going into battle, sometimes felling the hosts before him, sometimes conquering himself, and, as we have already seen, leaving the battle wounded. After Diomedes had struck the god, he went to Olympos shrouded in a mist, had himself healed by Paieon, and complained to Zeus about Athena, who had brought this defamation upon him, but Zeus did not hear his complaint. Athena herself also once threw him to the earth with a heavy stone, so that he fell to the ground under the clash of arms and covered with his great body seven mornings of land, and when Aphrodite wanted to carry him away from the battle, Athena struck her on the breast with her powerful hand, so that she too fell to the earth. With Heracles he was twice engaged in hand-to-hand combat. The first time Ares attacked the hero after he had killed his son Kyknos. He ran at Heracles with his spear, but Athena turned it away and the hero was then able to reach the god with his sword. The second time Zeus separated his two warring sons with his lightning.

The sons of Aloeus, the Aloids Othos and Ephialtes, overpowered the fierce god, captivated him and kept him imprisoned in a copper vessel for thirteen months, until Hermes managed to free him by trickery.
Although Ares, in the Greek imagination, was the wildest and most untamable of all the Olympian gods, and the bringer of death, pestilence and all kinds of unfortunate calamities, it was also said of him that he enjoyed the most tender love of the charming Aphrodite.

It is well-known from the Odyssey the myth that both were once ambushed by the crippled Hephaistos, Aphrodite's lawful consort, cunningly caught in an artful net and abandoned to the mockery of all the gods.

Ares' children

The most famous child of this clandestine union was the afterwards married Harmonia, the divine Unction, with Kadmos. As this one possessed the loveliness of the mother, so the sons Deimos and Phobos, who, it is said, had sprung from the same union, had the disposition of their father. Eros and Anteros are also said to have sprung from this parental pair. Ares possessed no legitimate wife, but he begot from mortal women and nymphs a multitude of children, among whom were excellent heroes. Also the dragon slain by Kadmos was born of the union of Ares with the Boeotian spring nymph Tilphossa. His son Kyknos he fathered with Pelopia or Pyrene. With Enyo he begot Enyalios. The twins Lykastos and Parrhasios, whom he had by Philonome, were to be the first rulers of Arkadia. Chryse gave him his son Phlegyas. By Triteia he had a son Melanippos (Pope., VII 22.8.).

Ares' companions

When he puts on his magnificent armor, his two sons Deimos and Phobos (Fear and Terror) bring him his golden chariot. They always accompany their father, while the discordant Eris, whom Homer calls the sister and friend of the man-killing Ares (βροτολοιγός / brotoloigós), speeds ahead of the murderous god's chariot. Enyo, the city destroyer, after whom he himself is also called "Enyalios" (Ἐνυάλιος), is also perpetually at his side. Kydoimos, a personification of the hubbub of battle, was also always featured in his entourage.

Ares' attributes

Ares had a *quadriga* drawn by four fire-breathing immortal stallions topped with golden scalps (*Iliad* V 352.). Among the gods, Ares was distinguished by his bold armor. He also swung his spear in battle. His sacred birds were the barn owl, woodpeckers and mainly the vulture. Also dedicated to Ares were the wolf, the horse, the boar and the cock (see Alectryo).

According to the *Argonautica* (II 382 ff and 1031ff; Hyginus, *Fabulae* 30), the "birds of Ares" (*Ornithes Areioi*) were a flock of feather-dropping birds that guarded the god's shrine with the Amazons on a coastal island in the Black Sea. In Sparta, the chthonic nocturnal sacrifice of a puppy to Enyalios was adapted to the cult of Ares.

In classical Greek art, his usual attributes were a helmet with shield and a lance.

Ares in the arts

The fact that the artists tried to give this god a beautiful form and thus give a proper expression to the Ideas of the Greek people, can already be seen from the fact that he was imagined as the god most loved by Aphrodite. Most of the statues that remain of him show him with milder features than one would expect of the barbaric, rough god of war, because they interpret precisely this most poetic feature of the myth of Ares, that he, the wildest, the most untamable of all gods, had to bow before the magic power of the goddess of love.

37

His hair is usually frizzy and short, his eyes small, his nostrils wide open - a sign of passion - and his neck and his entire body muscular. He is usually depicted beardless; only the oldest sculptors have represented him with a beard. His entire physique and posture indicate strength.

Among the tragedy poets, Ares also appears as the god of all calamity, of infectious diseases and miscreants. Later writers make him participate in the battle of the Giants. After first killing some of them, he finally had to take the form of a fish to remain hidden from the great Typhoeus, who persecuted him.

Some traits of the Greek Ares are found in the essence of the Roman war god Mars.

Artemis

The goddess of the hunt and of wild animals and vegetation

The ancient Romans identified her with their goddess Diana.

Artemis (Ancient Greek: Ἄρτεμις) is a goddess of Greek mythology. She was then among the twelve gods of the Greek Pantheon, where she is a daughter of the chief god Zeus and Leto and twin sister of Apollo. Artemis was equated by the Romans with their goddess Diana.

Birth

When Hera, the wife of Zeus, discovered that Leto was pregnant by her husband, Hera banished Leto to the floating island of Delos. The island was surrounded by swans. Artemis was born first and then helped her mother give birth to Apollo.

Hera's revenge was sweet. She made Leto suffer for nine days and nine nights at the birth of Apollo. There are several versions of this story. For example, according to the *Homeric hymn to Apollo* (3) Leto wandered past all kinds of regions and islands, which, however, did not dare to receive her. Finally she arrived at Delos, to which she prophesied that a temple of Apollo would bring wealth to the island. At this, Delos allowed Leto to give birth to her children there.

Hunting Goddess

Artemis is the goddess of hunting, women and also goddess of the moon. Her oldest function was that of ruler of game, a god type that was especially widespread in the Middle Eastern areas, but already Homer describes her as the goddess of hunting. She is depicted with a silver bow and arrow (made by Hephaistos), with a doe beside her, and also often with the moon. Sometimes the moon is depicted on her forehead with two small points (the points of the just-new moon, which also looks like a bow). Accompanied by her nymphs, she traversed the mountains and forests of Arcadia and Lacedaemonia; of the animals, the doe and the bear were especially dear to her. Other attributes belonging to Artemis are the goose, wild dogs and especially on Delos also the olive tree. The nickname of Artemis is Dhelia, named after the island of Delos.

Artemis is also the goddess for the pregnant woman, although she herself always remained a virgin. Virgin she remained by her own free will, for which, moreover, her father Zeus gave permission. Her priestesses are therefore unmarried women. Artemis was especially worshipped in wooded Arcadia. As a virgin, she was also the patron goddess of chastity.

Trojan War

Artemis was at the beginning of the Trojan War because she made sure there was no wind when Agamemnon wanted to set sail to go to Troy. This was because his men had killed a doe dedicated to Artemis. Artemis forced Agamemnon to sacrifice his daughter Iphigenia to get a favorable wind. Odysseus got the idea to send a letter to Clytaimnestra and her children that Iphigenia would be allowed to marry Achilles. The family came immediately and there had to hear the news that someone had to be sacrificed. This of course aroused the anger of his wife Klytaimnestra. This fact was again at the beginning of the legends surrounding Orestes. At the last moment, however, Artemis saved the girl and a deer was sacrificed in her place. Iphigenia was taken away by Artemis to a place far away from her family (who meanwhile also thought their daughter was dead), she became priestess of Artemis. After the Trojan War, Klytaimnestra killed Agamemnon in his bath because she had never forgiven him.

Attributes

Artemis is similar in many ways to her younger twin brother; Apollo. They both had a bow and arrow with arrows that never missed. She is also often depicted with a deer/deer.

Niobe

Besides being a huntress, Artemis was in many ways the spitting image of her brother Apollo: she too acted punitively against lawbreakers and killed them with her arrows. Famous is the story of how she and her twin brother Apollo killed the children of Niobe, because the latter boasted that she had more children than Artemis' mother Leto. Apollo killed Niobe her seven sons, and Artemis her seven daughters

Aktaion

The hunter Aktaion had fifty hunting dogs. One day he went hunting with his dogs. When he was thirsty he went to drink from a stream, but in doing so he accidentally saw Artemis who was bathing there naked, surrounded by her nymphs. Artemis saw that Aktaion was spying on her and turned him into a deer. The deer Aktaion ran away, but he failed to escape from his own hounds and he died a horrible death.

Orion

The hunter Orion shot them dead with her arrow. The most common story tells that Artemis and Orion loved each other. Her jealous twin brother Apollo could not stomach that his virgin sister had a lover and tricked her, so she killed Orion thinking he was some kind of hunting animal. She later gave Orion a place among the stars and gave him her favorite hunting dog Sirius.

According to another story, Artemis killed Orion when he tried to rape her. She killed many others who tried to rape her or other women.

According to yet another story, Artemis sent him a poisonous scorpion after Orion boasted of destroying all the animals on the earth.

The *Bibliotheca* of pseudo-Apollodorus of Athens says of the affair with Orion:

Artemis killed Orion on Delos. They say he was born of the earth and had a huge body; but Pherecydes calls him a son of Poseidon and Euryale. Poseidon gave him the ability to walk on the sea. First he married Side, who was cast into the realm of Hades by Hera after a dispute over beauty. Later, when he came to Chios, he courted Merope, the daughter of Oenopion. But Oenopion got him drunk and blinded him in his sleep, after which he threw him on the beach. However, he went to the smithy of Hephaestus, kidnapped a boy there, placed him on his shoulders, and ordered him to indicate how to walk to the sunrise. When he got there, the healing effect of the sun's rays restored the light to his eyes and he turned back at lightning speed to avenge himself on Oenopion. But Poseidon had had a home made for him under the earth by Hephaestus. Eos fell in love with Orion and abducted him to Delos; in fact, Aphrodite made sure that she constantly lusted after him because Eos had shared bed with Ares. Orion, according to some, was killed when he challenged Artemis to a discus throwing contest, but others say he was shot with arrows by Artemis when he tried to rape Opis, one of the girls from the land of the Hyperboraeans who had joined her.

Athena

The goddess of war, wisdom and of crafts

The Romans identified their goddess Minerva with Athena.

Pallas Athena (also **Athena** or **Athene**) (Attic: Παλλὰς Ἀθηνᾶ, *Pallás Athêna*, Ἀθήνη, *Athénē*) is one of the principal goddesses of the Greek pantheon. She had several functions: she was goddess of controlled warfare and peace. She was also goddess of wisdom (philosophy), civilization, the political community of the city and protector of several Greek cities, especially Athens. She was also patron goddess of artisans (crafts, such as weaving) and artists.

In mythology, she is known as Athena *Parthenos* (the Virgin) and the Parthenon was dedicated to her.

Etymology and origin

Athena's name is possibly of Lydian origin. It is possibly a compound word, derived in part from the Tyrrhenian "ati," meaning "mother," and the name of the Hurritic goddess "Hannahanna," which was often shortened to

43

"Ana." In Mycenaean, she possibly appears in a single inscription on Linear B tablets: *A-ta-na-po-ti-nin-ja /Athana potniya/* appears in a text from the Late Minoan II "Chamber of the Chariot Tablets" at Knossos, which is the very earliest Linear B archive. Although this is often translated as "Mistress Athena," it literally means "*potnia* of At(h)ana," possibly meaning "lady of At(h)ana"; but it is unclear whether there is a connection to the city of Athens. We likewise find *A-ta-no-dju-wa-ja /Athana diwya/*, the latter part of which is the Linear B spelling of what we know from Ancient Greek as *Diwia* (Mycenaean *di-u-ja* or *di-wi-ja*), the so-called "divine" Athena, who was also a weaver and goddess of crafts (see *dyeus*).

In his dialogue *Cratylus*, Plato gives the etymology of Athena's name based on the view of the ancient Athenians, from *A-theo-noa* (Α-θεο-νόα) or *E-theo-noa* (Η-θεο-νόα) meaning "the spirit of God" (*Cratylus* 407b). Plato, as well as Herodotus, noted that the Egyptian inhabitants of Saïs in Egypt worshiped a goddess whose Egyptian name was Neith; they identified her with Athena (*Timaeus* 21e), (*Histories* II 170-175.).

Neith (literally "weaver," meaning "I have come from within myself") was a war and protection goddess and mother of the crocodile god Sobek. Neith was also called Anatha and Ath-enna. Neith was the spirit behind the veil that no mortal could see directly.

The goddess was closely associated with Attica and Athens and enjoyed the greatest veneration there, but this did not exclude that her worship was spread throughout Greece. Almost every landscape assigned her an important role in its legends, Argos in those of Perseus and Diomedes, Corinth in those of Bellerophon. Especially also the landscape of Boeotia was distinguished by the great veneration given to the goddess (there was also a city called Athens). At Lake Kopaïs, especially in the city of Alalkomenai, her worship was held in high esteem from the most ancient times. Many of her most famous temples were also found on the coasts of Asia Minor, in the Trojan land and in Lydia. In short, wherever Greeks had settled, whether in Asia or in Libya, in Italy or in Sicily, Athena was venerated as a worthy, martial and beneficent goddess.

Pallas Athena

As for her name, one seems to have to distinguish between Athena and Pallas Athena, as she is very often called among the poets Hesiodos and Homeros.

The name *Pallas* seems to have been originally inserted as a praedicative adjective before Athena, designating her as the lance-wielding goddess, a symbolic representation of her power over lightning. Her *epiklese* Pallas (Παλλάς / *Pallás*) probably comes from the Greek verb pallein (παλλειν / *Pallein*; "to swing the lance") and thus means something like "she who swings the lance."

The name may also be related to Pallas, a friend of Athena or the giant Pallas, who was defeated by Athena during the Gigantomachy.

Origin myths

Also the myths, which relate to the origin of Athena, denote her as a goddess, who possesses a tremendous power over all the phenomena of the heavens, but also as a lovely goddess, who spreads blessing everywhere by making the fields fertile, multiplying and educating the genus of men, and all this without giving up anything of her wholly single purity.

Athena Tritogeneia

Regarding the origin of the goddess, several myths were circulating. An ancient nickname of Athena was *Tritogeneia*. This name designates her as a goddess born of water, and this is quite natural, since according to Homer all things and all gods owe their origin to water. The mass of water, which was called Triton, and was represented in one myth as a lake, and in another as a river. Sometimes the place was imagined to be in Boeotia, sometimes in Thessaly, yes, most people even imagined it to be in Africa, in Libya, where Athena was supposed to have risen from the waters. This idea was based on the fact that out of and through the water rising from the depths, the air, the sky and all the wonderful phenomena that occur in the sky were created, and as a result, Athena was most often or at least very often worshipped at the banks of lakes or rivers. This was especially the case in Boeotia, for example in the already mentioned city of Alalkomenai. Also in Arcadia and in Lydia, which was completely closed off from the rest of Greece by mountains, this Athena *Tritogeneia*, the goddess who emerged from the waters, was held in the highest esteem.

Athena Obrimopatrê

An entirely different myth concerning her birth has pushed this first one completely into the background. Already the *Iliad* of Homer knows Athena as the dearest daughter of Zeus. She is the one of his children who enjoys

45

his greatest confidence; all the difficulties, which Zeus has to overcome, are overcome by her deeds. Zeus speaks to her as to himself. The two of them are one. She is therefore called *Obrimopatrê*, "the daughter of a strong father." This close relationship between Athena and Zeus is symbolically expressed by the most famous story circulating among the Greeks concerning her birth, namely, that she would have been born of her father.

Zeus, according to this saga, had devoured his first consort, the goddess and Titan Metis (this is "the sagacious one"), the daughter of Okeanos and Tethys, because he feared that she would bear him, after a daughter, a son, who would again snatch from him the world dominion, which he had acquired with so much effort. As a result of this act, after some time he gave birth to Athena or Pallas Athena, who emerged from his head mature and armed. When the time came for her to see the light of day, Hephaistos had to split Zeus' head open in order to relieve him of an unbearable headache, and now she emerged from it with her lance raised, singing a war song. A tremendous upheaval in nature, a violent earthquake and an equally violent roaring of the sea accompanied the birth of *Pallas* Athena, who was also to be the great goddess of war. She was worshipped as a goddess of war as early as Minoan times (3rd millennium BCE - 1200 BCE).

Since Athena emerged in full armor from the head of Zeus, she is thus naturally destined to be goddess of war; but she is not equal to the fierce Ares. She protects the state, which is engaged in war, when that war must serve to legitimately repel the attack of strangers, or also, when it is undertaken for the sake of higher interests and a skillful and wise direction of the war can bring benefit to the state. Athena, in contrast to Ares, "represents the battle conducted with mastery, reason and strategic insight.

Does she lay down her arms, then there is peace on earth. The myth indicates this by telling that as soon as she, having stepped out of her father's head, bent the raised lance to the earth, the sky cleared. On the island of Rhodes, people knew to speak of a golden rain, which Zeus had poured out on the island at her birth, which of course is a symbolic expression for the descending of the pure light of the *aether* on the earth.

Athena glaukios

Athena *glaukios* is a nickname often given to Athena by the poets. *Glaukopis*, this is "the goddess with brilliant eyes," and the owl, who shares this characteristic with her, and is always represented as her faithful companion, also refer to the luminous goddess of the pure, clear *aether*.

Athena Promachos

If we now pay attention to the meaning of Athena as an ethical goddess, if we examine her relations to the life and work of men, then we must first consider her as a goddess of war. It is mainly the older hymns and sagas, which highlight this trait of her being. With a huge statue she was honored on the Acropolis of Athens as Athena Promachos, i. e. as the goddess who would protect and defend the city even in battle. In Boeotia, in Macedonia, she was especially the goddess of war, to whom people paid homage. She is often mentioned next to Ares. The greatest heroes of antiquity were under her constant protection. Perseus and Bellerophon, the Aetolian Tydeus, Iason descended from the tribe of the Minyers and the national *heros* of all Greece, Heracles, all enjoyed her support and protection. In the Trojan War she stood faithfully by the side of Achilleus, Diomedes and Odysseus.

Sometimes she climbs the chariot with the heroes, felling with her lance everything that stands in her way, even making those gods give way who are inferior in strength to her. Her courage always stays with her, but not less her presence of mind; even in the utmost danger she remains calm and fearless. Although the goddess participates in battle as fanatically as Ares, Athena is more concerned with strategies, rather than just gross bloodshed. And when the battle ends and the danger passes, she refreshes and strengthens and rewards the heroes, whom she loves and who have behaved worthily to her.

Goddess of art

Athena also enjoyed great honor as a goddess of the works and arts of peace, making those who honored her and especially her favorite country happy. She did this first of all by caring for the physical well-being of the inhabitants. Especially in the saga of Erichthonios, reference is made to the double blessing she bestowed on Attica through the thriving of the fruits and the glorious growth of the ephebia. She is thus the protector of the ephebia. Yes more than that. A visit by her priestess was reckoned to promote marriage. Young children were hung serpents made of gold in memory of the miraculous history of Erichthonios. She had taken these from Gaia (the Earth), his mother, to care for and nurse him. In the same way, she continues to care for the children. On Delos, people knew how she had assisted Leto when the latter gave birth to Apollo and Artemis.

Athena was also goddess of crafts, such as weaving. The myth of Arachne is related to this.

Athena Hygieia

But as goddess of clear skies and clean, healthy air, she was also revered as Athena *Hygieia*, the health bringing goddess. Diseases were warded off by her. She ensured the preservation and propagation of the human race. At the time of Perikles, a statue is said to have been dedicated to her for the recovery of a sculptor who had fallen off a scaffold while working on the Parthenon.

Athena Polias

And while thus the household, the family, was under her care, she naturally thereby also became the goddess who protects and guards the greater union of the people, the state, which the household is based upon. *Polias* was her name in that capacity, not only in Athens, where the Ancient Temple of Athena was dedicated to her, but also in several other places of Greece. By her the members of the *Boulè* in Athens swore their oaths on the altar dedicated to her, also called the Great Athena Altar. The earliest reference to the altar concerns the year 632 BCE.

The Parthenon was her main sanctuary, from *parthenos* (virgin).

Like a good spirit, she was present in the *ekklèsia*. The ancient court of the Areopagos had been founded by her, and by that foundation she had succeeded in reconciling the Erinyes, who had formerly been goddesses of vengeance, and made them Eumenides, benevolent deities, who wished to spread blessing and prosperity over the land. The *Areiopagos* acquitted Orestes of the murder of his mother Clytaimnestra.

Even where Greek tribes were more closely united by an alliance, it was Athena who stood at the head of such an alliance, supporting and protecting it everywhere with advice and action.

Furthermore, people attributed to Athena the introduction of some certain branches of culture and of some arts. First of all, mention must be made of the cultivation of the olive tree. Linked to its cultivation is the legend of the struggle Athena had with Poseidon over the possession of Attica. When

48

they quarreled over this possession, Zeus determined that the landscape should be assigned to the one who would endow it with the most useful gift. Poseidon then created either the (wild) horse or, by striking the earth with his trident, a source of salt (or brackish) water, Athena the olive tree. The gods awarded the prize to Athena and since that time the olive tree was sanctified to her above all other trees. The tree, which she had brought into being, stood in the immediate vicinity of the Erechtheion and had a life force, which could not be destroyed.

When the Persians burned the temple and the tree after the conquest of the city by Xerxes, new trees immediately sprouted from the ground. Certain olive trees dedicated to the goddess were also found in other places in Attica; for example, in the Akademeia, a garden located a short distance from Athena, there were twelve olive trees, which either owed their existence directly to Athena or were thought to be shoots from the olive tree on the Acropolis. Everywhere outside Attica, too, this tree was sanctified to Athena.

Athena Erganê

Because of the various arts, whose introduction was attributed to her, she was given the nickname of *Erganê*, i.e. "well experienced in all arts" - one was mainly referring to weaving and spinning. Homer mentions many times the artistic works of Athena, ornate clothes, which she had made either for herself or for the heroes she protected. From this arose in Asia Minor the legend of her contest with Arachne, who had tried to compete with the goddess in skill and had been transformed into a spider as a punishment.

From here also, that the greatest gift, which was brought to her annually by the Athenians, consisted in a beautifully crafted garment (*peplos*). Also the Trojan women - the service of the Trojan Athena, by the way, had very much in common with the Greek one - in order to reconcile the goddess offered her the cleanest of their clothes.

But not only did she teach men to spin and weave, she also gave them the rake and the plow and taught them to use the bull in farming; all artful labor, especially that spent in the manufacture of female ornaments had their origin in Athena; yes, even the carpenter, the goldsmith, the wheelwright, the potter and the ship's carpenter could not lack her help. The Roman poet Ovid added the follower, the painter, the shoemaker, to indicate that all artists and all artisans should receive help and support from her.

Furthermore, she was attributed inventions in the fields of music and dance. She had first played the flute and Lydia and Boeotia competed for the honor of having first heard its tones. A legend, which perhaps owed its genesis to this rivalry, told that Athena had abandoned flute playing, when she had seen in the waters of a stream, that the inflating of her cheeks disfigured her countenance. The flute thrown away by her was found and taken by the Silenced Marsyas. When he began to play her, however, he was punished by Athena.

She had also invented the warrior's trumpet. Also a martial dance, the *pyrrhic*, which she herself had first danced in celebration of the victory over the Giants and which was therefore performed in her honor every year at the Panathenaeans.

Goddess of wisdom

Finally, she, the goddess of the pure, clear *aether*, is also the goddess of clarity of mind, of calm and calm deliberation. That is precisely why she is the patron goddess of the thoughtful and resourceful Odysseus, that is why, in the battle between Achilles and Agamemnon, she comes to exhort the former to calmness and composure, that is why she has become the goddess of sages and of all practitioners of science. This trait in her being was especially prominent in Athens. This can be explained by the great purity and clarity of the air of Attica, which also acted favorably on the faculties of the mind. It was also this quality that bound Athena to her father Zeus by the closest ties. She is, as it were, the personification of Zeus' sagacity. However, this does not prevent her from sometimes participating in cunning schemes forged against her father.

Relationship with other gods and mortals

Hephaistos

One of the oldest legends the Athenians knew how to tell about their goddess was about Hephaistos' love for her. Although the goddess rejected the god's proposals, the god's ardent desire to possess her gave rise to a being, half snake and half man, named Erechtheus or Erichthonios. The germ, which once would give birth to this being, was, so the story goes, enveloped by Athena in a fleece of wool and thrown down to earth. It is clear that we are dealing here with a figurative representation of a very ordinary natural phenomenon. From the hot bottom of the earth, symbolically represented here by Hephaistos, impure vapors rise to the pure *aether*. This is not defiled by them, but they remain shrouded in a woolly cloud, hanging below until they descend again to earth as fertilizing rain.

Ares

There is a great difference between her and Ares, the god of fierce battle. Athena is not interested in fighting: she does not rush like a senseless brute into the wildest fray, but calmness, deliberation, determination grant her victory when she goes to war in defense of sacred rights or to achieve a noble goal. In this respect she is the opposite of Aphrodite. Athena is the powerful, strong goddess, while Aphrodite is the powerless goddess who does not understand the art of war. This Athena always brings victory. She is therefore almost identical with Nike, the goddess of victory. Athena once won a war from Ares, which settled their relationship.

Poseidon

She is also worshipped alongside Poseidon, because like him she is one deity who delights in those who devote themselves to seafaring and in those who know how to tame the impetuous power of the horse and make it subservient to themselves. As *Hippia*, the goddess of horses and horsemen, she was worshipped on a hill in Kolonos, a place in the immediate vicinity of Athens; on the southern tip of Attica, on the promontory of Cape Soenion, she was honored as the patron goddess of those who sail the sea. In Athens she had taught Erichthonios how to harness the horses; in Corinth they told how she had shown Bellerophon how to tame the winged horse Pegasus. In various places she and Poseidon were praised as the deities who took charge of horse breeding and taught man how to serve the horse. She made herself known as the protector of seafarers when she built for Danaos the ship with fifty oars with which he fled from Egypt to Greece. Likewise, when she built or helped build the Argo, the ship with which Jason and his went out to retrieve the Golden Fleece from Colchis. Even the horse of Troy, which was built by or at the advice of Athena and became the means by which the Greeks finally entered the city, relates to this side of the goddess' being. Of course, all these representations were immediately related to the clouds, which show themselves on the *aether* and are so often compared to fast horses or swift ships. After Athena caught Poseidon and Medusa in her temple, she is said to have made the latter turn her into a gorgon and this further settled the relationship with Poseidon.

Aphrodite

Because, as below, Aphrodite got the golden apple and not Athena, their relationship is bad. Also, Aphrodite does not like the fact that Athena is a virgin. Once when Athena found Aphrodite behind a loom she became furious because she thought that weaving was too beautiful a craft and that it was defiled when Aphrodite did it. It is said that Aphrodite never did anything even remotely resembling work after that.

Trojan War

Athena took sides against the Trojans in the Trojan War because she could not forgive Paris for not awarding her the golden apple, which was destined for the most beautiful of goddesses. Consequently, not only Paris, but also all his countrymen, suffered constantly from her hatred and persecution. In this war, fought by mortals, but provoked by strife among the gods, Athena even turned against some of her fellow gods, who sided with the Trojans in the battle.

Yet Athena was also worshipped in Troy. The Trojans possessed the wooden *Palladion* and as long as they held that statue of Athena, Troy remained invincible. However, Odysseus and Diomedes managed to capture the statue. In the aftermath of the war, Kassandra sought shelter with another statue of Athena, which was toppled by Ajax. This outrage caused a significant portion of the Greek expeditionary army a disastrous retreat. Poseidon hampered Odysseus' retreat, while the "shrewd" hero continued to enjoy Athena's support during his journey back to Ithaca.

Children of Athena

Athena is virginal, but can also have children with mortals (humans). She often gave those children as gifts to her new love. Athena could have her children born from her head, keeping her virgin. All of Athena's children are hated by spiders because Athena turned the then mortal weaver Arachne into a spider.

When Athena was besieged by Hephaistos, she successfully fended him off, but his seed fell on her thigh. She wiped off the seed and it fell to the ground. From the fertilized earth, Erichthonius was born. Athena adopted him as a son and entrusted him, in a basket of Attic wickerwork, to the three daughters of Cecrops: Herse, Pandrosos and Aglauros. They were not allowed to look inside the basket, but Aglauros undid the knots and inside the basket they saw a baby with a snake monster beside him. Aglauros was later driven to jealousy by Athena and turned to stone by Hermes.

52

Non-Greek influences on the statue of Athena

To what extent the service of the Egyptian goddess Neith or Phoenician mythology influenced the original formation and development of the representations of the Greeks concerning *Pallas* Athena is difficult to determine. What is certain is that the figure of Athena, as she is portrayed to us in the poems of Homer, possesses a genuine, peculiarly Greek character and no traces of foreign influence can be recognized in it.

Athena worship dates back to ancient times; the name is un-Greek and cannot be satisfactorily explained, nor can some of the ancient honorary titles worn by the goddess in Homer's epics. Her character is ambiguous: she was, on the one hand, the martial damsel, goddess of war, who supported the valiant, orderly struggle in defense of homeland and law, leading the way in battle and bestowing victory; legendary heroes such as Achilles, Diomedes and Odysseus were under her care.

On the other hand, Athena was the goddess of prosperity and peace, the giver of all that characterizes civilized society. She upheld law and justice, was the protector of the public assembly and taught men how to wield the plow and fire and how to put horses in front of wagons; in addition to art and science, female handiwork was especially dear to her.

Attributes and symbols

The same metaphorical representation, which underlies these accounts of the birth of Athena, is also found in her principal attributes and symbols, the *Aegis* and the *Gorgoneion*; the *Aegis*, the shield, or armor, or mantle, jointly possessed by Zeus and Athena, the Gorgoneion, the head of the Gorgo Medusa placed in the middle of it, both representations of the dense cloud, which contains thunder and lightning, and thus also of the darkness, out of which light is born. Although the head of Gorgo obtained its place on the Aigis, which belonged to Zeus, it was nevertheless given to Athena by Perseus and was therefore one of the attributes, without which the goddess was never thought or represented. This is especially true of the representation of the goddess at Athens, and in the first place on the Acropolis of Athens, the fortress of the city, which has long been devoted entirely to the service of this goddess. On the southern wall of the Acropolis one saw a large, gilded Medusa head on an *Aigis*, which served to indicate the terror with which Athena, as *Promachos*, as the patron goddess of her favorite city, would drive the enemies from her walls.

The owl, snake and rooster were also sanctified to her. The olive tree was dedicated to her.

Athena is depicted in full armor, with aegis (skin of a goat with snakes attached), helmet, shield, sword and/or spear. Medusa's head is worn on aegis, breast cuirass or shield.

Parties

The close relationship, in which she stands to that *aether*, is also evident from the symbolic ceremonies at several of her festivals. Nowhere were these festivals (*Panathenaia*) celebrated in greater numbers and with more splendor than in Attica, especially at Athens. On the Acropolis she had two temples, called the Erechtheion, and the Parthenon. Significant remains of both are still preserved to our time. In the Erechtheion they kept the oldest wooden statue of Athena, said to have fallen from heaven, and the memorials of her battle with Poseidon for possession of the landscape of Attica. The Parthenon, as its name indicated, was the temple of the "virgin goddess." There was her most famous statue, made by Pheidias (c. 431 B.C.), among other sculptures, the state funds and the state archives.

It goes without saying, that Athena as goddess of nature exercised a great influence on agriculture, on the thriving of the seed, and was therefore invoked in various ways during the year and honored with various festivals. During the sowing season, although Demeter was honored primarily, of the three sacred plows, with which the sign was given, that the sowing season had arrived, two were dedicated to Athena (*Skiras* and *Polias* respectively). Even when the fruit was germinating, people turned to Athena for further blessing. Furthermore, by a whole series of ceremonies and customs, mostly of a somber nature, through purifications and atonements, the help of the deities of the *aether* was implored against the scorching heat of the sun's rays in the summer time. These included the Plynteries and Kallynteries, which were celebrated in the month of *Thargelion* (May). Then the *peplos*, the beautifully crafted robe, was taken off the ancient statue of the goddess and the statue itself was washed, a ceremony by which was meant not only cleansing, but also the humidity so necessary at that time for the seed fields. In July, people celebrated the Skirophoria. Then the statue of Athena was covered with plaster, with lime clay. Then a great procession was held, in which the priests and priestesses wore large sunshades, to turn away the glowing sun heat. Thus, on this feast, too, people sought protection from Athena against the evil effects of the scorching rays of the sun. Likewise, the feast of the Ersephoria or Arrephoria (for which the Arrephorion was built) was connected with Athena as goddess of nature, and this can also be said of the greatest feast celebrated in honor of the goddess in Athens at the time of the harvest, of the Panathenaeans. In this festival, which was not even remotely equaled in splendor by any of the others, the ethical significance of Athena gradually came to the fore. Yet even here the gifts she had bestowed as goddess of nature remained in memory, especially the gift of the olive tree. Old men and women carried olive branches in their hands at the solemn procession held on the occasion of the Panathenaeans, and those who had triumphed in the contest at this feast were wreathed with olive branches from the sacred tree and received as a reward amphorae extracted with oil from that tree. Finally, at the time of the vintage among the Oschophorians, in addition to the deities that viticulture was more particularly dear to the heart, Athena was also gratefully remembered as the goddess who bestowed blessing and fertility on the entire landscape.

The visual arts

In all regions inhabited by Greeks, the goddess was frequently depicted. Of the older statues, whose pose did not yet possess the looseness and naturalness of the later Ancient Greek works of art, some depicted the goddess seated, as the goddess of peace, usually with a spinning wheel at her side. Other statues showed her with raised lance and outstretched shield as the goddess of war. Such images were commonly called *Palladians*. On their constant possession depended the salvation and preservation of the state. Such a *Palladion* was stolen from the Trojans by Odysseus with the help of Diomedes.

Athens, Argos, most cities of lower Italy, but also Rome boasted of possessing such a *Palladion*. These statues, it was said, had fallen from heaven, and concerning their finding and the eccentric fates and wanderings of some of them a great number of legends were in circulation.

Among those older statues can also be counted the Athena statue, which was found near the goddess' temple on the island of Egina in 1811 and is currently kept in the glyptotheque at Munich.

How well the image of Athena was known to all Greeks, at least to all Athenians, is shown by the story that Peisistratos, expelled from Athens, had himself brought back into the city on a chariot, seated beside a woman adorned with all the attributes of the goddess Athena, and that the Athenians took him in, thinking that their goddess herself had brought him back.

The later, more beautiful statues of Athena were all of the type designed by the great sculptor Pheidias. Three statues of Athena created by this sculptor attracted particular attention in classical antiquity, first of all the statue in the Parthenon, made of gold and ivory, secondly the huge bronze statue of Athena *Promachos* on the Acropolis, which was made from the spoils obtained at Marathon, and finally a bronze statue, which was erected by Athenian colonists on the island of Lemnos and was therefore called the Lemnian Athena. The gracefulness of this statue was so great that people there used to call the goddess "the beautiful one." It represented Athena as the artful goddess of peace.

The busts, statues and images of later Greek art can also be divided into two main groups, one representing the goddess as a goddess of war, the other giving her the attributes appropriate to Athena *Erganê*.

Demeter

The goddess of agriculture

The Romans identified their goddess Ceres with Demeter.

Demeter (Ancient Greek: Δημήτηρ, *Dêmétêr*) is a figure from Greek mythology. She was the daughter of Kronos and Rhea and thus a sister of Zeus, Poseidon, Hades, Hera and Hestia. Demeter was the goddess of agriculture and crops (primarily grain). She is often depicted holding an ear of corn. The Roman equivalent of Demeter is Ceres.

Origin

After her birth, according to Greek mythology, she shared the fate of her siblings: she was devoured by her father Kronos, but, like the others, recalled to life when Zeus forced his father to regurgitate the children he devoured.

The goddess Demeter, literally invoked as a *divine mother*, possesses all the characteristics of the older Cybele, a Phrygian goddess, who in turn was a reflection of the goddess Kubaba from Hattic mythology.

Demeter Pelasgis

The conception of Demeter as the mother earth belongs to her original being. She is closely related to Gaia and Rhea Cybele, although she nevertheless has a different personality. One can safely hold her for one of the oldest, Pelasgic (pre-Hellenic Greece) deities of Greece, hence her nickname *Pelasgis*. What some writers have claimed about her Egyptian origins and about her identity with the Egyptian goddess Isis seems implausible.Demeter was the sister of Poseidon and the sister-in-law of Hera. But Demeter secretly had a crush on Zeus. Hera knew this and did everything in her power to destroy her.

Demeter's scope of work, epikleses and worship

As goddess of the earth, she is primarily associated with everything related to life and human civilization. She became the goddess of agriculture, and once she was this, of course, also of all those pursuits that can be included in a broader sense of agriculture, arboriculture and animal husbandry.

The goddess of agriculture further became the protector of everything related to agriculture. She passed for the inventor of all the tools used in it. She also taught people plowing, sowing, mowing, tying sheaves, threshing, grinding and baking bread, according to the myth of Triptolemos (see below).

Demeter Thesmophoros

As the goddess of civilization, who raises people above the level of hunters and shepherds through farming, Demeter also has a moral significance. With this she is closely related to Dionysos, the god is, who gave civilization to the human race.

Offerings

To Demeter they sacrificed the pigs detrimental to corn, as well as cattle, fruits, honey and honeycombs. In addition to all fruit trees, the pine, elm and of the flowers hyacinth and the poppy were dedicated to her.

Parties

In addition to the Eleusinias and Thesmophorias, several other great festivals were celebrated in honor of Demeter, mostly related to the harvest. The principal places of her worship, besides Eleusis, were Crete, Delos, Arcadia, Attica, Anatolia and Sicily.

The Dorian tribes devoted themselves for the most part to the service of Apollo and Artemis, and therefore that of Demeter took a back seat with them, although it also seems that this goddess is of ancient, truly Greek origin.

Children

Demeter enjoyed the love of the supreme god Zeus and had a daughter, Persephone, with him. In addition, she gave birth to Despoina and the sea god Poseidon fathered the horse Areion with her. Furthermore, she gave birth to the sons Ploutos and Philomelus through Iasion.

Dionysus

The Romans called this god Bacchus and celebrated the Bacchanalia, or festival of Bacchus, every third year. It became so immoral, however, that in 186 bc the Roman Senate forbade it.

Dionysos (Ancient Greek: Διόνυσος, *Diónysos*; Διώνυσος, *Diṓnysos*; Latin: Dionysus) or **Bakchos** (Greek: Βάκχος, *Bákchos*; Latin: Bacchus), sometimes also **Iakchos** (Greek: Ἴακχος; Latin: Iacchus), or **Bromios**, is a figure from Phrygian, Thracian and Greek mythology. He is the god of wine (construction) and fruit growing, the growing power of the earth, of laws, human civilization, spirit and enthusiasm, poetry, theater and music. As god of peace, he brings people together and as victor over death. He had an important influence on the life, thought and work of the Greeks and Romans in several ways.

Parents, birth and youth

Dionysos was the son of Zeus and Semele, the daughter of the Theban king Kadmos. The love Zeus harbored for Semele greatly aroused the jealousy of Hera. She went to Semele under a false guise (Beroë) and persuaded her to ask Zeus, as proof that he was truly the god of heaven, to show himself to her in all his glory. Bound by an oath, Zeus had to grant the foolish request, but when he came to the unfortunate in the full blaze of his lightning, she burned with her house.

Zeus, however, saved the child she carried in her womb, and immediately ivy vines sprang up from the pillars of the palace, protecting the child with their cool leaves. Zeus hid his son in his thigh until the time of his birth would have come, and when Dionysos came into the world for the second time, he handed him over to the nymphs of Nysa for care and education. Originally that was a mythical place; later several regions of Greece bore that name. There the child was raised under the faithful care of the nymphs.

Another lore mentions Ino, the sister of his mother Semele, as his educator, and let him join the nymphs first, after she too had had to succumb to Hera's persecutions.

In Phrygia and Lydia there was also the saga, different from the original Greek story, that the god would have been entrusted to Rheia-Kybele for his education.

When he was grown up, he planted a vine and with the drink extracted from it he intoxicated himself and his educators and the demons of the forest. Everyone who came into contact with him was seduced by the sweet fragrance of the new drink and joined the procession, with which Dionysos traveled through the world to spread the wine, new gift, which he wished to bestow on mankind.

Features

He is a god whose influence extends over a very wide area. He was revered primarily as the god of wine. Wine was the finest of his gifts and it was therefore also called Διόνυσου καρπός, Diónysou karpós, Dionysos' fruit. But there is more. He also meant to the ancient Greeks the power of growth, which can be seen in nature, for example of the forests, fields and trees. The mountains and springs there are also connected with it. Therefore, the wine grape is only the fruit, which is associated with him as a god. The grape, though born of moisture, gives a warm glow to its fruit. The weakness and courage, the lushness and strength, of which the grape is the symbol, are the symbol of Dionysos.

61

But also all trees and all tree fruits were under his care. All moist places were therefore sacred by him, especially the soil that was fertile. Many springs were dedicated to him. He could also make springs flow from rocks by striking them with his thyrsos staff, not only water, but also wine, milk and honey.

Viticulture and fruit growing are found only in peoples who have reached a certain level of development. Hence, Dionysos became a god of human civilization. He was closely associated with Demeter in this way. He gave people their laws, maintained peace and showed them his favor through his good gifts. Viticulture and agriculture were seen as the gifts of Dionysos and Demeter especially in Attica. There the saga of Ikarios, to whom Dionysos bestowed his gift, and of Triptolemos, who was chosen by Demeter to be her envoy, originated.

Dionysos also influenced the human mind; he brought people together. Whatever resisted him had to bow before his power. All that was wild and rough submitted to him: panthers and lions pulled his chariot and the most ferocious deities of nature willingly joined his retinue. He was the god of élan and enthusiasm. This expressed itself especially in the fields of poetry and music. The poetry and music dedicated to Dionysos are fierce, they are characterized by sudden transitions from the most exuberant joy to the deepest sorrow. The festivals dedicated to Dionysos were quite noisy because of both the songs, the dithyramben, actually the songs that celebrated the double birth of Dionysos, and the musical instruments used in them, the flute and the tambourine.

Dionysos, moreover, was a god of prophecy and purification, and therefore connected with Demeter and with the deities worshipped in the mysteries of Eleusis. In them he was called Iakchos, a name for his loudness. The name Bacchus later adopted by the Romans, Bakchos, seems to have the same meaning, also his nickname Bromios seems to refer to the noise with which his feasts were accompanied.

He was also associated with the underworld as victor over death and was equated with Hades by Herakleitos.

Dionysos' wanderings

The legends tell that he was welcomed especially in Aetolia and Attica. In Aetolia, Dionysos had taken up residence with Oineus (= "the wine man") and had a love affair with his wife Althaia. According to some, the beautiful Deianeira was the god's daughter. Much more detailed and important is the story of Dionysus' arrival in Attica. Two places claimed to have taken in the god first: Eleutherai and Ikaria. Eleutherai, however, had been annexed to the territory of Attica only later, so the Dionysos of Ikaria was and remained the truly national deity. His arrival there is recounted in the following legend: Ikaros, the ruler of Ikaria, when he asked for hospitality, kindly accepted the god. In gratitude, Dionysos gave him the vine and taught him viticulture. When Ikaros had won the first wine, he filled leather sacks with it and traveled through the land to distribute that delicious drink to the shepherds. These, however, soon became drunk and, believing they had been poisoned, they killed Ikaros and buried him under a tree. His daughter Erigone went out to look for him and finally found his grave with the help of her faithful dog Maira. Despairing of her father's murder, she hung herself from the tree under which he was buried. Dionysos was enraged by the murder of his friend and sent a plague across the land. He made all the Attic damsels follow Erigone's example in fury and made Ikaros the constellation Boötes and Erigone the constellation Virgo. The dog Maira he placed in the sky as the Dog Star.

The meaning of this myth is clear: Ikaros is the personification of the vine, Erigone (= "the one born early") means the grape, and the dog is the heat of the dog days, which brings the fruit to maturity.

Feasts and worship

The disasters that had come upon Attica after the death of Ikaros could not, according to an oracle, cease until the corpse of the murdered was found and a sacrifice was made for the crime. The dead body was not found, but a feast was instituted in fulfillment of the oracle's demands, at which all sorts of small statues were hung from trees and rocked to and fro while singing songs in honor of Ikaros and Erigone. This festival was called Aiora, and nowhere was it celebrated with such pomp and splendor as in Attica, especially in Athens. But these festivals were celebrated among all the Ionians, even those who inhabited the coast of Asia Minor in great numbers.

Winter Festivals

The Attic festivals are partly harvest festivals in winter, partly festivals of the approaching spring. The actual feast of the vintage was celebrated on the "little Dionysia," which was celebrated in the month of *Poseideon* (December-January) in the country, that is, outside the city of Athens. Songs in honor of Ikaros and Erigone were sung, there was dancing, and the symbolism of fertility bestowed by Dionysos was carried around with loud jubilation, and merriment was everywhere. In those rural Dionysians lies the first origin of Athenian drama. Chariots carried singers who recounted the fortunes of the god in a dialogue, and even later, when the Athenian drama had already reached its highest stage of development, actors from the city still traveled around to add lustre to the rural Dionysians through their performances. A peculiar entertainment, which was very popular, was the Askolia: boys limped around on an oil-coated leather sack made from the skin of the goat slaughtered in honor of Dionysus.

The rural Dionysians were followed by the Lenaies in the month of *Gamelion* (January - February). That feast was celebrated in the city as a conclusion to the previous one. Mainly, it was celebrated in the *Lenaion*, the oldest temple, which Dionysos had in Athens. Grapes were festively pressed and the young sweet must, called *ambrosia*, was tasted and sacrificed. People and temples were wreathed with ivy; there was a great procession, in which, especially from chariots, all kinds of mockery and jest were given to the assembled crowd; theatrical performances concluded the feast.

Spring Festival

When spring began, people celebrated *Anthesteria* in the month of *Anthesterion* (February - March). Each day of this feast had its own significance. The first day, the *Pithoigia*, was the feast of the breaking of the barrels of new wine. On that day, slaves were free and equal to their masters. The second day, *Choën* was celebrated with a meal, for which the state provided the meat and prizes were awarded for those who could drink the most of the young wine. The first flowers of spring were used for wreaths for the people and for the Lenaion. The *Anthesteries* were also celebrated by the children. From their third year, children were wreathed on that day as a personification of the young year. An important part of the *Anthesteries* was an offering made to the god on the day of the *Choën* by the noblest women of the city at the Lenaion. In the process, the wife of the *archon basileus*, or the official in charge of governing the religion, was united in marriage under mysterious ceremonies. This was probably a symbolic repetition of the union made around the same time of year between Dionysus and Ariadne.

The third day of the *Anthesteries* bore the name of *Chytren* (i. e. "the festival of pots"). Then sacrifices were offered to the phantoms of the dead, who used to return to the upper world on this day in order to receive the gifts due to them, and to the chthonic Hermes, who guides the phantoms. The explanation of this sacrifice lies in the fact that at the
64

awakening of nature in spring, in addition to the return of Dionysus, i.e. the force of growth of nature, from the realm of the dead to a new life, one also celebrated the awakening of all that had once lived and seemed to have died.

Dionysia

The fourth festival, the real spring festival, that the Athenians celebrated, were the *great Dionysians*, the *Dionysians in the city*. The month of *Elaphebolion* (March-April) was the month designated for these feasts. Taking part in them was allowed even to prisoners, because on this feast people celebrated the god especially as the liberator of care and suffering. The most distinctive feature of the great Dionysians was the wonderful theatrical performances given in honor of the god. A very large crowd of people flocked to Athens from far and wide. Then a merry crowd went back and forth through the streets of the city. The festival began with a magnificent procession, which accompanied the oldest statue of the god found in Athens. Numerous choirs sang in honor of the god especially the *dithyrambos*, i. e. the song, in which his double birth was sung. People wreathed themselves with roses and violets, the young flowers of spring. But the main point of the whole feast was and remained the performance of new tragedies and comedies, during which a competition was held between the various poets. The choice of those who would be allowed to compete was made beforehand from among those who had applied. The influx of foreigners was so great and the revelry of the citizens was so full of all moods, that these days were chosen as the most appropriate for the state to award honorary degrees to deserving citizens.

Oschophoria

But not only in Attica and Athens was the service of Dionysos in such high honor. Also on the island of Naxos they knew many stories of the god. There it was, that he had found Ariadne, when the latter had been faithlessly abandoned by Theseus. It is a favorite subject of the poets to sing of the nameless grief of Ariadne in her desolate state and the blissful joy that filled her, when she was chosen by Dionysus for a wife.

At Athens they celebrated a feast in their honor, the Oschophoria, which was also a harvest festival, at which sons of Athenian citizens dressed in ancient Ionian costumes carried around vines with grapes hanging from them in a solemn procession. From the marriage of Dionysos and Ariadne sprang three sons, Oinopion (i. e. "the wine drinker"), Staphylos (i. e. "the vine") and Euanthes (i. e. "the clean bloomer").

Opponents

Everywhere Dionysus went he spread blessings. Only those he ruined who tried to resist him. First of all the Tyrrhenian pirates, who wanted to take him as a prisoner. Indeed, when he was about to sail from Ikaria to Naxos and was wandering on the beach, Tyrrhenian pirates captured him, as he attracted attention because of his extraordinary beauty. But hardly was the ship in the sea, or the shackles which had been put on him fell off, vines grew around the sails, ivy clasped the mast, and the robbers plunged into the sea in a fit of madness and were turned into dolphins.

More than once Dionysos had enemies to fight, as the legends of Lykurgos and Pentheus prove. Lykurgos, the son of Dryas, was a king of the Thracian Edonians. When the god had entered his realm with all his attendant multitude, he went to meet them with hostility, in order to discipline the intruder and if possible kill him. The intruder, however, saved himself by jumping into the sea, where the goddess Thetis took him in. Lykurgos, however, was punished with blindness, and having incurred the hatred of the gods, he soon had to die. Other legends tell that, having become insane, he either mistook his son for a vine and killed him with his axe or, overcome by such blindness, cut off his own legs. It seems that Lykurgos is a symbol of the chilly winter, which tries to disturb the joy of the god of vigor, but has to succumb again and again in the unequal struggle.

In the Boeotic saga, Pentheus occupies the same place as Lykurgos in that of northern Greece. He is called a king of Thebes and is described as a man of gruff and fierce nature. When Dionysos also visited Thebes on his journey through the world, all the Theban women gathered around him and celebrated a noisy feast in his honor on the mountains of the Kithairon. Angered by this, Pentheus wanted to put an end to this, but when he wanted to attend one of the secret ceremonies held on the mountains unnoticed and had climbed a pine tree for that purpose, he was torn apart by his own mother, who mistook him for a wild animal, with the help of her companions.

From this saga concerning the Boeotic Dionysos, it is already clear that his worship and his festivals in some regions of Greece were of an entirely different character from those celebrated in Athens. Fierce and noisy feasts they were, in which women and girls participated in overwhelming numbers, as appears from the legend, which relates to the daughters of King Minyas at *Orchomenos*. Proud of all admonitions and miracle signs, these alone of all the women of that city refused to take part in the feast in honor of Dionysos, until at last the god, followed by the fierce multitude that surrounded him, entered their house, and when he found her there laboring, had it overgrown with vines and ivy wreaths and turned them themselves into bats.

The legend tells of many battles in which Dionysus is said to have been involved; he is said to have fought with the Amazons, there is mention of a battle he fought against Perseus, but especially famous is the part he played in the victory of the gods over the Giants. The mother of these great beings, who wanted to storm the heavens, Gaia, had made them invulnerable to the weapons of the gods, so that they could continue their battle unharmed, until two beings, in whose veins also flowed the blood of mortal men, Dionysus and Heracles, were called to their aid by the gods and ensured them the victory.

Trieteric festivals

Especially on the Parnassos near the city of Delphi, noisy festivals were celebrated. Even women from Attica went there to participate. In the darkness of the night they would wander around on the snow-covered peaks of the mountains, sometimes risking their lives, and tear apart everything that came into their hands, deer and other game, to devour the still trembling flesh raw. A deafening noise caused by the screams of the revelers, accompanied by the music of flutes and tambourines, was a peculiar feature of these parades over the mountains. Such Dionysos festivals were celebrated every other (the Greeks said every third) year and were therefore called *trieteric* festivals. The cause of this excitement can be explained by the significance of Dionysos as a god of nature. At the time of the winter solstice the grape seems to die away completely, as it were, and the god, it was thought, died with the plant sanctified to him. Hence a sadness, which is similarly found in all nature religions, where man sees in the dying away of nature the image of his own dying, and which gave itself air in all kinds of wild and excited customs. On the other hand, there were the feasts of joy, with which the god was greeted when he was reborn in the spring, and the noise with which the women who took part in these feasts went over the mountains, which served to awaken the god from his death sleep. They searched for him everywhere until they found him, i.e. his symbol, a newly germinating plant; then they brought it in solemn procession to his temple to conclude the feast with sacrifices and dancing.

Mainaden

On her journey over the mountains, the women were dressed in animal skins, and carried a thyrsos staff (i. e. a stick wrapped with ivy and vines) in their hands. They were called her Mainaden, Bakchanten, Thyiaden, Bassarides. (See Bassareus.) These savage festivals had their origin mainly in Thrace and Makedonia, whence they were transferred to Greece proper, especially to Boeotia, among which the Dionysos festivals, the *Agrionies*, i. e. "the savage festival" in Orchomenos held a first place.

These Mainads were also in the representation of the Greeks part of the great procession, which surrounded the god on the journey he had undertaken to spread his gift. That procession, called *thiasos* by the Greeks, and the subject of numerous representations of the visual arts, was composed of very different components. While at first only Nymphs had been the companions of the god, he was soon surrounded by all sorts of groups of Silenes, Satyrs, Pans, Kentaurs and other beings of such nature. Needless to say, his old teacher Silenos was not absent from these surroundings. With that whole multitude he passed through all lands, planting the vine everywhere and establishing his worship. His journey, on which he, as it were, subjected the whole world to himself, was extended by the ancient writers as far as India. Especially as a result of the campaigns undertaken by Alexander the Great, this journey became more prominent among the later Greeks under the legends of Dionysus. Alexander favored the view, as it were, that he wanted to continue the enterprise of Dionysos and penetrate even further than there, where the traces of the god and his worship reached. It goes without saying, that all the countries, in which the service of Dionysos had taken root in later times, were included in the descriptions of that journey, and numerous sagas and stories of adventures, native to different countries, were gradually united into a whole. Especially the Asia Minor landscapes of Phrygia and Lydia must be counted among those regions, where Dionysos had long sojourned and founded an enduring worship, which, like other worship in those regions, bore a ferocious, excited, as the Greeks said, *orgiastic* character. There the god was surrounded by the ordinary companions of Rhea Kybele, the *great mother of the gods*, namely by the Curets, by the Korybanten, Kabeiren and Idaiian Daktylen.

In Lydia or in Phrygia, the saga of Ampelos also originated. This was a beautiful youth, whom Dionysos had met and loved on his wanderings. Always Ampelos was the god's faithful companion, until a bull killed him. Dionysos was distraught with grief, so Zeus, to relieve that grief, sprouted a vine from the blood of Ampelos.

Access to the Olympos

Precisely because Dionysos was only partially of divine origin, he had to be cleansed of all that clung to him before he could enter the circle of the Olympian gods. After the journey he had undertaken over the whole earth, by which he had subjected all nations, as it were, to his territory, he entered victoriously into the dwellings of the Olympos, where he was henceforth granted residence. And once there, he managed to arrange for his mother Semele, according to some legends even Ariadne, to be assigned a place on Olympos as well. Semele received the name of Thyone. Hence the not infrequently given name of *Thyoneus* to Dionysus.

Mysteries of Orphici

We find a very peculiar conception of the nature of the god among the Orphici, a religious and philosophical sect, which named itself after the mythical singer Orpheus from Thrace, and set itself the task of spreading clearer notions about life after death and about the moral responsibility which rests on every human being for his acts and omissions. In the mysteries of those Orphici, the main deity was Dionysos-Zagreus. This deity, called either the son of Zeus and Demeter, or sprung from Zeus' union with his own daughter Persephone (a saga, which tried to symbolically represent the influence of the forces of heaven on plant growth) is, according to the Orphici, the darling of his father, appointed by the latter to rule the universe. Therefore, Zeus made him king and, already when he was young, gave him more honors than to the other gods. His education in his childhood was entrusted to the Curets. But Hera, who persecuted all the sons of Zeus who were not hers with an evil hatred, sent the Titans upon the child, having ordered them to render their countenance unrecognizable by smearing it with chalk. Although the child transformed himself into various forms by his divine power, he was finally forced to succumb in the unequal battle. The Titans tore his body apart and devoured it. Only his heart was saved by Athena, who brought it to Zeus.

Two different sagas tell, that either Zeus himself devoured this heart, or, that he gave it to Semele, the mother of Dionysos. Either from Zeus himself, or by his doing, the younger Dionysus is then born, who would be the king, the liberator, the salvation of the world. The Titans, however, who had torn Zagreus apart, were struck by Zeus' lightning to such an extent that they burned to ashes. From these ashes, which were mixed with the blood of Zagreus, human beings were born. And it is precisely from this that the human character can be explained. The lust for evil, which every man carries with him, finds its origin in the ashes of the Titans; the inclination to do good springs from the blood of Zagreus mixed under those ashes. In short, the duel between good and evil, which prevails in every human mind, is symbolically represented by the mixing of what is Titanic, i. e. fierce and crude, and what is Dionysian, i. e. good, pure and clean.

The teachings of the Orphici were proclaimed in a secret worship service, in so-called mysteries.

A secret worship service, which can be called the Dionysian Mysteries, also seems to have been in vogue at the trieric festivals of Dionysos.

Distribution

The worship of the Greek Dionysos was also spread beyond the borders of Greece. Especially in those Greek colonies, which covered Sicily and the coasts of southern Italy, he had a great expansion. In Rome, though under other names, many temples were founded in the god's honor. But that worship of the Romans was soon completely estranged from the original Greek worship in many respects. First of all, what contributed to this was that the new deity, which was introduced in Italy in a very explainable way, was linked as closely as possible to ancient, native deities. Secondly, the ceremonies associated with his service soon became a cover for such gross immorality in the Bacchanalia, which has remained proverbially infamous until today, that the authorities of the city had to act in the strongest possible way to prevent a general decay.On the worship of Dionysus in Rome, see Liber Pater and *Senatusconsultum de Bacchanalibus.*

Relationship with other deities

To some other deities Dionysos stood in a more or less close relationship. His relationship to Demeter has already been discussed. With Apollo he had several points of contact. It seems that in the beginning these two deities were hostile to each other and that it took a long time for the Dionysian service to gain a place next to that of Apollo. The noisy celebrations of Dionysus were too much of a contrast to the service of the pure god of light, which was dignified and measured in everything. Yet even this struggle once came to an end. Points of similarity were found, which made it possible that in the representation of the Greeks these two gods were closely connected. Like Apollo, Dionysos knows how to arouse in people's minds enthusiasm for what is beautiful; both are equally friends with the Muses. Like Apollo, Dionysos is also a prophetic god, and he too, as will be shown, granted people cleansing from sin and guilt.

In the visual arts

A great influence did this Asia Minor worship have on the representation of the god by the visual arts. The numerous images depicting him as a youth of frail, almost effeminate stature, whose richly abundant wavy locks are bound together by the Lydian hairband (*mitra*), are also of Asia Minor origin. Often the god is dressed in wide, fur-colored clothing, while he is sometimes depicted as a youth, sometimes as a man of more mature age with a full beard.

None of the Greek gods has so often been the object of representations in the visual arts as Dionysus, and with no other god is the variety of these representations greater. Sometimes he is depicted as a child, sometimes as a youth, sometimes as a mature and powerful man; sometimes with a languorous, almost feminine appearance, sometimes brought into a state of rapture by the most violent movement of the mind; sometimes drinking, sometimes riding on wild animals, usually surrounded by Ariadne, Silenos and his entire thiasos.

The oldest images of the god were very simple; a piece of wood representing him, an image of his face alone were often enough to ignite his worshippers in enthusiasm.

Herms have even survived, representing either the head of Dionysus alone, or next to his own that of the deities most closely associated with him, whose image then seems to sprout with him from one tree trunk. Later art found in the legends related to Dionysus and his environment a very rich material for its works. Especially the sculptors Skopas and Praxiteles (both lived in Athens from about 392 - 350 B.C.) and their pupils tried to glorify the god in the most different states and environments through their images.

Dionysos as sacrifice

According to the legend of Dionysos as a peace offering, he was fathered by Zeus with Demeter. Zeus already placed him on his throne as a youth where he played with the thunder boulder. The Titans (who had been defeated by Zeus) watched this with displeasure and, in the absence of the Alfather, they ambushed Dionysus. Who tried to escape by shapeshifting, but in the form of a bull was finally seized, torn to pieces and eaten.

However, the goddess Athena saw it and preserved the heart. She brought it to Zeus, who resurrected his son with it. In the cult of the god Dionysos, a bull was slaughtered every year, the blood of which was drunk and the meat eaten. Dionysos was also the god of theater; from his dithyrambe, tragedy was born.

Hades

The god of the underworld, the underground dwelling place of the dead

---

*The counterpart of Hades in Roman mythology was
known as Dis or Pluto.*

Hades (Ancient Greek: Ἅδης), also **Haides** (Ἀΐδης), **Ploutoon** (Πλούτων),
Plouteus (Πλουτεύς) or **Pluto**, **Orcus**, **Dis Pater** (Latin) is a figure from
Greek mythology. He is the god of the underworld or Phantom Kingdom
and ruler of the dead. Also, he is the god of wealth and precious metals.
Hades is a son of Kronos and Rhea and the husband of Persephone.

Figure (god)

Hades is a brother of Zeus, Poseidon, Hera, Hestia and Demeter. In the
division of power and world between Zeus, Poseidon and himself, the
subterranean kingdom of the dead fell to him, making him the third world
ruler. Hades suffered the same fate as his brothers and sisters (except
Zeus): he was eaten by his father Kronos and later spat out again. Also,

he participated in the Titans' battle at the side of Zeus. He does not allow anyone to return to the realm of the living. Several demons and spirits are in his service, such as Charon the ferryman who uses his boat to ferry the souls of deceased people across the river Styx on payment of an obool (a coin placed in the mouth of the deceased for this purpose).

The attributes of Hades are the two-tooth and Kerberos, the monstrous three-headed dog that guards the entrance to the Underworld. Furthermore, Hades also sometimes carries a bag of money, as he was also sometimes honored as a god of wealth. This is also derived from his name: Ploutoon/Pluto (πλουτος = wealth). Hades also got a helmet that could make him invisible from the cyclopes.Hades loved Persephone, daughter of the goddess Demeter, and kidnapped her. Of the heroes, Heracles, Orpheus, Odysseus, Peirithoös and Theseus descended into the underworld while still alive. Homer describes the dark realm and its dejection.Hades was also nicknamed "Nil miserans" (ruthless, unmerciful, knowing no pity) by Horace, yet the god of the underworld had once taken pity on Orpheus, and his wife Eurydice.

Underworld

Hades also refers to the underworld, both in Roman mythology and Greek mythology.

The underworld had as its most gruesome part *Tartaros*, here the ghosts or spirits of the dead were sent if they had lived badly. Examples include Sisyphos and Tantalos, who when they died had to endure eternal torments.

A lovelier part of the underworld was the *Elysion*. This was the place where anyone who had led a good life could enjoy freedom and peace. According to the stories, this is where Aeneas meets his father Anchises.

The third and final part of the underworld was a place without hope or fear. Here all were sent who had led normal average lives, neither good nor bad. This place was called the Asphodel or the fields of Asphodel, named after an edible plant that was very neutral in taste. Whoever ended up here was allowed to fly and roam around as a bat for the rest of eternity.

Hephaestus

God of fire and metalworking

The Romans identified their god Vulcan with Hephaestus.

Hephaistos (Ancient Greek: Ἥφαιστος) or **Vulcanus** (Latin) is a figure from Greek mythology. He is the god of forging, fire and craftsmen and is blacksmith of the gods. According to some sources (Homer, et al.) he was the son of Zeus and Hera, according to others (Hesiod) he was only the son of Hera.

The Romans equated him with their god Vulcanus (also called Mulciber). He was married to Aphrodite, but Aphrodite cheated on him with her lover Ares, the god of war. From Ares she had a child named Harmonia.

Mythology

He had strong arms, like any blacksmith, and underdeveloped legs. Hephaistos, however, was also limp. In Homer's *Iliad*, his appearance to the gods elicits "Homeric laughter. Two explanations exist for his limp. According to one, Hephaistos was present at a marital dispute between his parents and when he intervened to defend his mother, his father grabbed him by a leg and threw him down from Olympus. A people from Thrace, the Sintians, who had ended up on Lemnos with a migration of people (that is where Hephaistos had come down in his fall), nursed him but he remained limping.

The other version says that Hephaistos was limp from birth, and that Hera threw him off Olympus out of shame, leaving him limping for the rest of his life. He ended up in the ocean, where he was fished out by Tethys and Eurynome who raised him in a deep large dark cave by the sea. When he had grown up, he decided to avenge himself by giving his mother a golden throne he had forged. However, when she took her seat on it, she was suddenly chained to it and no one but Hephaistos could free her. Both of the above stories are found in the Iliad.

It is also said that Zeus, in order to get on good terms with Hephaistos after his return to Olympus, decided to give him Aphrodite as a wife. Although he himself was ugly, Hephaistos always had beautiful wives: apart from Aphrodite, mention is made of Charis, described as "graceful," and of Aglaea, the youngest of the three Graces. Of the sons of Hephaistos, the Argonaut Palaemon, the sculptor Ardalus, the robber Periphetes, who was killed by Theseus, and Erichthonios are especially well known.

Relationships

Aphrodite was not happily married to Hephaistos. She loved Ares and Ares loved her. While Hephaistos went to work in his workshop on Olympus, Aphrodite secretly allowed Ares into her bed. Hephaistos knew from the moment he married Aphrodite that this was going to happen. As cunning as he was, he devised a plan to show the world that Aphrodite was cheating. He created an invisible net that would fall over Aphrodite and Ares when he wanted it. He also invited all the gods to come. The plan worked and Aphrodite and Ares, while naked, became entangled in the net. All the gods started laughing when they saw them. Hephaistos eventually freed them.

Another story states that Hephaistos had fallen in love with Pallas Athena. Hephaistos allegedly ran at Athena naked and his seed got on Athena's clothes. Athena allegedly wiped it off with a cloth and threw the cloth into a valley. As a result, mother earth, Gaia, became fertilized. The resulting child was named Erechtheus. He would later be the first king of the city of Athens.

Attica, a daughter of Zeus and Eurynome, is said to have married Hephaistos. Together they had four beautiful daughters, also called the Charites. Hephaistos is also said to have had another brief relationship with a nymph. From this a number of divine daughters would also have been born.

Cult

Hephaistos was originally worshipped in Asia Minor (Lycia) as a demon of all kinds of natural fire phenomena. From there his cult came to the island of Lemnos. From the island of Lemnos, the Hephaistos cult came to Athens, where the god became the protector of potters. The Temple of Hephaistos was built next to the quarter of these artisans.

Incidentally, all the workings of fire were associated with Hephaistos. Under the volcanoes he had his workshop, as under the Mosychlos on Lemnos, where the Cabeirs were his helpers, and in the west under the Stromboli, but chiefly under Etna, where the cyclopes served him. In Homer's Iliad, his name is directly linked to fire, where the fire over which meat is prepared is occasionally referred to as the "flame of Hephaistos.

He forged weapons and equipment for gods and heroes, for example, Poseidon's trident, Heracles' shield and Achilles' cuirass. Prometheus was forged by him and the beautiful Pandora was his creation. An artist in blacksmithing, he was in close relationship with Athena, the goddess of the arts. In Athens, the festival the Chaldeia was celebrated for both gods together.

Iconography

The earliest known depiction of Hephaistos dates from the sixth century BC and shows the birth of Athena, as well as a scene with Peleus and the return to Olympos. He was usually depicted with typical blacksmith's tools such as the hammer, pliers and bellows. Numerous statues of the Roman equivalent of this Greek deity have been found, as well as sarcophagi and mosaics, among others.

Hera

Queen of the heavens and as the protector of marriage and women | Sky deity

The Romans identified their goddess Juno with Hera.

Hera (Ancient Greek: Ἥρα, *Hêra*; Ἥρη, *Hêrê*; Mycenaean: *e-ra*) is a goddess from Greek mythology. She is the daughter of the titans Kronos and Rhea, and thus the sister of Zeus, the king of heaven and earth, as well as being his wife. Hera was the goddess of marriage and fertility. She is also called the "cow-eyed one" and the peacock is her symbol.

Origin

Originally, Hera was only the patron goddess of marriage. Soon, however, she symbolized the air and atmosphere that brings fertility. She was seen as the mistress of heaven and earth. Her name means "mistress of all that exists." Like her consort, she is able to bring all kinds of weather phenomena such as thunder and lightning down upon the earth.

Being the spouse of the supreme god, she is treated with great reverence and respect by the other gods. Everyone stands up for her when she enters the hall.

There are several stories about Hera's childhood. One version is that she was raised by Okeanos and Tethys. According to another version, she was raised by the Horns. Unbeknownst to her parents, she entered into a sacred marriage ("hieros gamos" or "hierogameia") with Zeus, which remained a secret for 300 years, until Zeus was able to grant her her worthy place as queen of heaven.

Besides the fact that Zeus and Hera clearly feel love for each other according to the Greek poets, there is also a lot of marital strife between them. The Greeks saw this struggle of Hera reflected in the natural phenomena in their land, which were strongly influenced by the sea. From this point of view, one can also explain the saga in which Zeus, as punishment for Hera's persecution of Zeus' son Heracles, hangs Hera from the sky with two anvils at her feet (representing the earth and the sea) and on her arms golden shackles (the clouds colored by the sun).

Scope

Hera's field of action expressed itself both in her capacity as goddess of the early *polis* (and possibly even earlier in Mycenaean times) and in her capacity as goddess of marriage as consort of the supreme god.

Goddess of the early polis

Hera's spiritedness is also reflected in the Trojan War, in which she supports the Greeks. After all, the Trojan Paris had designated Aphrodite and not Hera or Athena as the most beautiful woman at the Paris Judgment. Even the Trojan Aeneas, who travels to Italy as a survivor after the Fall of Troy, still experiences Hera's resentment.

Marriage Goddess

Hera has further great significance as the goddess of ancient Greek marriage and is considered the ideal of the married woman. Her real is considered the model for every marriage made on earth, and marital fidelity is under her protection.

Children

The children who resulted from Hera's marriage to Zeus were Hephaistos, Ares, Hebe and Eileithyia. Hephaistos is said to have been born when the marriage of Zeus and Hera was also a secret to their parents. Hebe and

Eileithyia symbolize, respectively, the blossoming, youthful vitality and assistance to barren women.

Cult Places

Hera was especially honored in the city of Argos and the festivals celebrated there, Heraea, which were accompanied by public games. From here the service of the goddess spread throughout the Peloponnese, with temples in Olympia, Corinth, Tiryns and Perachora, among others. Argos and the nearby cities of Mykenai and Sparta are already mentioned by Homer as Hera's favorite cities. In addition, the Hera cult was central on the islands of Delos and on Samos, where Zeus and Hera are said to have secretly married. On Lacinium in southern present-day Italy, near Kroton, there was also a temple dedicated to her.

Attributes

The cow, and the peacock were dedicated to Hera, and especially the pomegranate as a symbol of life. She was often depicted with a peacock, a child or a staff. The peacock had in its tail the eyes of Argos, whom Hera had appointed as shepherd over the cow Io, into which one of Zeus' mistresses had been transformed. Argos was killed by Hermes and robbed of his eyes. Hera is protector of flocks and is called "cow-eyed" by Homer.

Hera in the visual arts

Hera is often depicted sitting on a throne, or dressed in a robe with a crown on her head. In her hand she very often holds a pomegranate, symbolizing fertility. A famous statue of Polykletos depicts her while sitting on a throne and wearing a crown decorated with the images of the Charites and the Horns. In one hand she holds a pomegranate, and in the other her scepter on which sits a cuckoo, another fertility symbol.

Hermes

God with numerous roles and the messenger of the gods

His counterpart in Roman mythology was Mercury.

Hermes (Ancient Greek: Ἑρμῆς, also *Hermeias* Ἑρμείας, Dorian: Ἑρμᾶς) is a figure from Greek mythology. He is a son of the chief god Zeus and the mountain nymph Maia and is particularly known as the god of trade, travelers, roads and thieves. He is also the messenger of the gods.

Originally he was a phallic deity and, coming from the pastoral land of Arcadia, Hermes was also the *nomios*, the grazing god, who protected shepherds and flocks. Later, however, many other qualities and attributes were attributed to Hermes. For example, he took over the task as messenger of the gods from Iris, which also made him Hermes Psychopompos: the soul companion who took souls to the underworld.

Because of his constant travels he became the patron of travelers, because of his athletic and youthful appearance he became the patron of athletes and sports, and because of his youthful escapades (see: Myths around Hermes) he became the patron of thieves. Because he constantly floated through the air using his winged attributes, Hermes became god of traffic and commerce, and his eloquence also earned Hermes reverence: he became the god of eloquence. Finally, Hermes was also considered the god of sleep and dreams: by touching his caduceus, he could put people to sleep and wake them up.

Hermes, however, was not only a highly athletic deity: later people even saw in him the inventor of writing, mathematics and astronomy. And all kinds of other useful and pleasant things were also attributed to Hermes, such as the lyre, flute and weights and measures. He was also patron of painters.

Mercury is often identified as the equivalent of Hermes in Roman mythology. However, this is not entirely correct. It is true that Mercury was inspired by Hermes; after all, he is the god of Commerce and also bears the attributes of Hermes. But the Greeks hardly revered Hermes as a god of trade; he was with them primarily the god of travelers and messenger of the gods. Thus, equating Hermes and Mercury is incorrect: the emphasis of the two gods is quite different.

Hermes and Apollo

Hermes was born in a cave in Arcadia. Shortly after his birth, he invented the lyre by stringing the shell of a tortoise with strings. Moments later, he escaped from his crib and snuck out of the cave. Not too much later, he came across a large group of cattle that belonged to Apollo. Hermes thought they were magnificent beasts and decided to take them with him.

A shepherd who was watching all this he forced to swear that he would never tell. The shepherd, named Battus, swore this to the young god, and Hermes continued on his way back to his birth cave. When Apollo discovered that his cattle had been stolen, he forced Battus to tell him who had stolen them.

Apollo went to the cave where by now Hermes was already in his crib and ordered him to return his cows. As Hermes and Apollo walked to where Hermes had hidden the cattle, Hermes played a tune on his lyre. Apollo became so impressed with the musical instrument that he asked Hermes to give him the instrument as a gift. In exchange for the lyre, however, Hermes asked for the herd of cattle, and thus the trade was born. For the shepherd Battus things did not end well, he was turned into a block of stone by Hermes because of his infidelity.

Later, the relationship between the brothers Hermes and Apollo improved considerably. Apollo even gave Hermes his caduceus, the snake-wrapped staff, which has been a permanent attribute of Hermes ever since.

Hermes and Argos

Once there was a beautiful nymph named Io who entered Hera's service as a maidservant. She was truly beautiful and Zeus soon took a fancy to her. Hera, who did realize that Io was a beautiful woman, slowly became jealous. To protect Io from Hera's jealousy, Zeus transformed her into a cow. However, Hera realized this and ordered Zeus to give her the cow as a gift, whereupon she gave the cow to the shepherd Argos. Argos was a giant with a hundred eyes and even when he slept he still had two eyes left to keep watch over his flock.

Despite this setback, Zeus did not sit back, but instead commissioned the clever Hermes to free Io. Hermes, unable to ignore a request from the supreme god, set out for Nemea, the city where Argos held Io captive. After a brief chat with Argos, Hermes played a tune on his flute, so soporific that even Argos' last two eyes closed. Hermes then cut off Argos' head and freed Io. When Hera noticed this, she sent a hornet that sent the poor cow running; Io ran throughout the land until finally she jumped into the sea at Epirus; this sea was later also called the Ionian Sea. In Egypt, Zeus returned Io to her normal form. Nor was Argos' dead body left untouched: Hera took all one hundred eyes and sprinkled them over the tail of her favorite peacock.

Hestia

Goddess of the hearth, home, and the family

Hestia is associated with the Roman goddess Vesta.

Hestia (Ancient Greek: Ἑστία, *Hestía*; Ionian: Ἱστία, *Istía*; also known as Ἑξία, **Hexía** and Ἑστρία, **Hestría**) is a figure from Greek mythology. She was the eldest daughter of Kronos and Rheia and thus also the eldest sister of Zeus. Yet in the popular belief of the Greeks, she was the youngest of the deities, who lived on Olympus, for in neither of Homer's poems is her name mentioned. As the eldest, she would be the first to be swallowed by her father (Kronos). and the last to be spat back out, so that at her "second birth" she was the youngest

Etymology and powers

Hestia is first and foremost the goddess of fire and more specifically the domestic hearth. Where no hearth is found, no cozy, regulated society is possible. This is therefore founded and promoted by her, and that both among gods and humans. Thus, when one also brings to the aid of the meaning of her name, one arrives at the explanation of what Hestia was as goddess of nature. Her name designates her as the goddess "who gives firmness." She is thus probably originally a personification of the earth, as the solid throne, on which the Olympian gods built their eternal dwellings and which is, as it were, the hearth of the universe, above which the fire of the ether burns.

Yet her significance as a goddess of nature in Greek mythology receded into the background altogether. The fire, of which Hestia was either the personification or the protector, soon meant a sacrificial fire, as it was found on the domestic hearth of every Greek home. On the domestic hearth, according to ancient, ancestral custom, every householder made offerings for the benefit of his family like a priest of the gods. Every special event in the life of the family gave rise to an offering, made to her. Thus one sacrificed to Hestia on going on a journey, on coming back, on taking new members into the household, even of slaves, especially on the birth of children, on the giving of the name, on marriage and on death. A special peculiarity of the domestic hearth, which is a strong proof of the great reverence, cherished for Hestia, lies in this, that as her altar it was an asylum, where the stranger, even the enemy found a safe refuge. All, who dwelt in the house and sacrificed at her altar, had equal claim to her protection. Moreover, Zeus had a weakness for his eldest sister and therefore punished all those who did not heed the pleas of a needy person. Thus, she also became the goddess of hospitality. Hestia is also said to have taught the art of building to man, when she saw that man had to shelter in caves from the rain, which her brother caused.

The household is the foundation of the state. So it goes without saying, that the goddess, who allowed herself to be worshipped at the center of the domestic circle, also became the protector of the state, that each state also had a common hearth, on which sacrifices were made to Hestia for the sake of common prosperity.

Various societies and brotherhoods, which emanated from the state, each had its own altar, on which sacrifices were made to the goddess, yet each state also had its own altar, which was dedicated to Hestia. That altar stood in the Prytaneion, originally the house, where the king lived, later the building, where the government was located. On that altar an eternal fire was maintained in honor of Hestia, and on the burning through of that fire depended the salvation of the state. It was a striking custom, that colonists who went from Greece to the foreign lands, took with them a part of the fire from the altar of Hestia, in order to light the fire on the altar erected in her honor in the Prytaneion of the *polis* which they were going to found, in order to maintain the close connection between *metropolis* and colony also by this worship.

And as much as each Greek state had its own altar and its own worship of Hestia, so also all Greece together had a separate sanctuary, dedicated to her. In the temple of Apollo at Delphi stood her most famous altar. That was the center of her worship. An eternal fire was also maintained there. It was believed that in the place where the altar of Hestia stood at Delphi, one saw not only the center, or as the Greeks put it, "the navel" of all Greece, but even of the entire earth. Whoever came to Delphi to seek counsel from the oracle began by offering his sacrifices on this altar. It was at that altar that Orestes was cleansed of his crime by Apollo. On that altar also sacrificed the singers, who hoped to receive from Apollo the gift of poetry. The fire, which burned there in honor of the goddess, was, according to the Greeks, as it were, the mirror image of the fire, which burned in the sacred hearth in the dwelling of Zeus on Olympus.

Pure and clean as fire is, was also the goddess' being. That is why she always remained a virgin. She had vowed to remain so, touching with her hand the head of Zeus, from which the virgin Athena had emerged. This is precisely the great distinction between her and Gaia, the all and all nurturing mother, who never ceases to give life to new beings.

In how high honor she stood with the Greeks, is also evident from this, that the saga told, that Apollo and Poseidon had vainly vied for her hand.

Hestia's worship service

However great was Hestia's standing among the Greeks, her worship was very simple. Temples to her alone were few, as every burning hearth and burning altar were her symbol. Many temples also had a separate altar erected for her. At large, solemn sacrifices, they usually began with an offering to Hestia, and she was also honored at the conclusion of the ceremony. According to an ancient legend, when the world was divided after the victory over the Titans, Hestia had desired for herself an eternal virginity and the firstfruits of all sacrifices. Thus, she received her share of every prayer, every religious act, every sacrifice, and every subsequent festive meal.

Her main cult sites were in Athens, Oropos, Hermione, Sparta, Olympia, Larissa and the island of Tenedos in the Aegean Sea.

Hestia in the visual arts

Obviously, the sculptors had to strive to make the goddess look serious, chaste and dignified. Sometimes she was depicted sitting, sometimes in a quiet, standing position. The most famous statue of the goddess from antiquity was in the Giustiniani Palace in Rome. The image to the right gives a representation of it. The face of the goddess has serious features. A close-fitting dress covers her entire body, her hair is made up in a very simple way, the back of her head and shoulders are covered with a veil. One hand is held against her side as a sign of calmness, the other points to heaven, which she represents on earth through her omnipresent power and activity.

Poseidon

The Romans identified their god Neptune with Poseidon.

In Greek mythology, **Poseidon** (Ancient Greek: Ποσειδῶν, *Poseidôn*; Doric: Ποτειδαν, *Poteidan*, Ποσειδάων, *Poseidáôn*) is the god who rules the sea, the waters and their gods. But he was also a god of horses and - as an "Earth Shaker" - of earthquakes. The Roman equivalent is Neptune. He is often depicted with a trident.

Origin

The name Poseidon, unlike that of most other gods, has an Indo-European derivation. The first part of his name is the vocative of Greek πόσις / pósis ("lawful husband") or Indo-European *pot- ("lord"): πόσει / pósei or πότει / pótei. The second part of his name is associated by some with δᾶ / dã ("earth") or -δᾶν / -dãn (cf. Zeus, "god").

In the surviving Linear B clay tablets, the name PO-SE-DA-O-NE ("Poseidon") occurs more frequently than DI-U-JA (Zeus), which seems to indicate that Poseidon was held in high regard by the Mycenaeans. However, we may need to nuance this because Poseidon seems to have been the principal god in Pylos, where a large number of these tablets have been recovered. A female variant, PO-SE-DE-IA, has also been found and presumably indicates a vanished partner goddess. Tablets from Pylos report offerings that were addressed to "the Two Queens and Poseidon" and to "the Two Queens and the King," although *wa-na-so-i* is considered by Chadwick to be a place or building. If the "Two Queens" refers to goddesses, it probably refers to the earth goddesses Demeter and Persephone or their predecessors, goddesses who in later periods were no longer associated with Poseidon.

Poseidon was already known as an "Earth Shaker" - E-NE-SI-DA-O-NE - in Mycenaean Knossos, a powerful attribute when one knows that earthquakes had accompanied the collapse of Minoan palace culture. Remarkably, no connection between Poseidon and the sea has yet been found in the very sea-dependent Mycenaean culture. This suggests that Poseidon was originally a chthonic god (that is, a god relating to the earth), who only later gained his authority over the sea.

This is also evident in the myths. Poseidon was born the son of Kronos and Rheia, from whom he also derived his epithet Kronios. He is said to have been devoured, along with his siblings, by his father, who vomited them out when his youngest son Zeus dethroned him. According to others, after his birth, Rhea hid him among a flock of lambs and his mother pretended to have given birth to a young horse, which she gave to Kronos to devour. A spring near Mantineia, where Poseidon is said to have been hidden, called *Arne* or "Lam(s spring)," is said to have derived its name from this. According to Ioannes Tzetzes, Poseidon's nurse bore the name Arne. When Kronos searched for his son, Arne is said to have said that she did not know where he was. From her, the city of Arne is said to have taken its name. According to others, however, he was raised by the Telchins at Rhea's request.

After the victory over the Titans and the establishment of the rule of Zeus, in the division of the world by fate, the sea had been assigned to Poseidon. He would thus have come into association with that element in a fortuitous way. However, this needs to be nuanced: although there was an important chthonic component to Poseidon's being, his connection with water in all his earthly forms was an equally essential part of him.

Worship

89

The worship of Poseidon in Greece was very general. Virtually all Greek tribes and all Greek landscapes were, albeit in different ways, closely related to him. First Thessaly, which owed its existence and its formation, as it were, to great floods and stormy earthquakes, where the god himself, by tearing apart the mountains, had provided the excess water with a passage to the sea, then Boeotia, which was so richly supplied with water and in part in its great water bowls, such as Lake Kopaïs, had experienced the god's influence to a great extent. Both countries were inhabited by the tribe of the Minyans, known for their chivalrous nature and lust for adventurous sea excursions. Further into the Peloponnese, where on Isthmos, created as it were for sea trade, with its great trading city of Corinth, the worship of the god, who could bestow all good gifts, but could also inflict the greatest calamities, as a matter of course occupied a prominent place in religious life. The narrow coastal strip, located at the northern end of the Peloponnese, was almost entirely the god's property. The temple of Poseidon on Isthmos also featured the first ship ever built, the Argo. There, after their glorious victories over the Persians, which laid the foundation for their naval power, the Greeks dedicated to him a colossal copper statue. But also in the interior of the Peloponnese, in Arkadia, where rivers sometimes disappeared underground, then suddenly reappeared, where subterranean basins were found in deep caves, Poseidon enjoyed great veneration.

In Troizen he was revered as *basileus* ("king") and it was there that he is said to have fathered Theseus, the later king of Athens. He was also revered as *wanax* ("king," "leader") in Corinth.

For the possession of Athens he had fought with the goddess Pallas Athena, and although he was also vanquished by the latter, he had left the marks of his sojourn. Still the place at the foot of the Acropolis is pointed out where he struck the earth with his trident. Yet in worship he appears as completely reconciled to Athena, and it was almost only the glorious sculpture on the gable surface of the Parthenon that preserved a memory of that battle. At Athens, therefore, a magnificent festival was celebrated in his honor, the Poseidon.

Likewise, the god's service was scattered throughout the Greek colonies. On the one hand, he was celebrated in the Ionian colonies, during the Panioni, held in his honor on the promontory of Mykale in Asia Minor, where the sanctuary of the Heliconic Poseidon is located. They considered this their greatest religious festival. In the Dorian colonies he was also worshipped, but here interference from, and confusion with, Eastern worship is not to be overlooked.It goes without saying, that to a god who was worshipped in so many places, very different characteristics and activities were attributed, and that not everywhere the same traits of his being were equally prominent.

The month of December/January, in which the sea reveals itself in its most impetuous power, was named after him *Poseideōn* (Ποσιδεών, later Ποσειδεών) in the Attic calendar. In the other Ancient Greek calendars, however, he had no month named after him.

Features

Poseidon's dwelling is not on Olympus, to which he does have access, but with his consort Amphitrite he resided in his golden palace at Aigai, located in the depths of the sea.

First of all, it should be pointed out that Poseidon belongs to those gods who lost their significance as gods of nature the earliest. Already among the oldest poets he appears as the ruler of the sea, nowhere as a personification of the sea itself. His power, however, is limited. According to Homer, he is the younger brother of Zeus, so that his subordination to him corresponds to the principles of patriarchal law. In contrast, with Hesiodos Zeus is the youngest of the sons of Kronos and Rheia, yet wiser and stronger than the predecessors. Poseidon lacks the lofty and impressive composure and sedation of the ruler of the heavens.

Though he is mighty and strong, he is as impetuous as the element over which he rules. If he thrusts his trident, which he always carries in his hand as a sign of his dignity, into the sea, the waves rise impetuously, crushing the ships and flooding the land far and wide. With the same trident, he can split rocks, cause earthquakes and raise islands from the sea. On the other hand, even one word, yes, one look from him is enough to calm the fiercest storm. When he on his golden chariot, with strong horses equipped with copper hooves, flies with the speed of the wind across the plain of the sea, then even the highest waves make a smooth path for him, and the monstrous monstrosities of the deep emerge and dance playfully around his chariot. To this characteristic of his being also belongs the struggles he had with other deities over the possession of regions or cities, such as with Pallas Athena over Athens (cf. *supra*) and Troizen, with Helios over Corinth, with Hera over Argos. A proof of his power are also the sea monsters, which he can conceive and which can only be satisfied by bloody sacrifices (e.g. Hesione and Andromeda.), the wild bulls, which come from the sea at his command to ravage the fields and kill the people, such as the Cretan or the Marathonian bull or like the bull that caused the death of Hippolytos.

91

On the other hand, by his power he is also the patron of all boatmen and fishermen. These pray to him for a happy voyage and rich fishing and they do not fail to offer him sacrifices in the success of their efforts. Sea warfare was also under his administration. He gave victory in naval battle. Therefore, all sea heroes pleaded to consider themselves his favorites, sometimes even his sons.

A second trait in the being of Poseidon is that he shook the earth but on the other hand also held and carried it with his powerful arms. When the gods took part in the battle for Troy, Zeus threw his lightning from the heavens, but Poseidon made the earth tremble, so that it shook on its foundations, and Aïdoneus, the prince of phantoms, feared that the sea god would tear off the lid of his dark realm and open it to the gaze of gods and men. So all earthquakes were attributed to him, and where large cracks or fissures were found in the rocks, where steep cliffs rose into the sea, there people thought they could recognize the traces of Poseidon's trident. Especially was this the case with the island of Nisyros, which, it was claimed, had been torn off from the island of Kos by Poseidon in the Gigantomachy and hurled at the head of one of the Giants.

Athens was not the only place where the god's trident had left three large openings in the earth as a sign of his presence.

He also often made islands rise out of the sea, such as Rhodes, Anaphe, Delos, and as a skillful master builder he made them rest on solid foundations, which were grounded in the seabed. So he also built the copper gates that closed the Tartaros, into which Zeus had cast the Titans and the Hekatoncheires. Likewise, he assisted King Laomedon of Troy in building the walls of his city and punished him severely when he would not pay the stipulated wages for labor. This faithlessness of the king made Poseidon the enemy of the Trojans forever.

Poseidon is also the god who gives fertility to the land, who spreads blessing through the springs and rivers which he creates, yes sometimes gives springs, whose water can cure the sick. Especially in regions that were usually poor in water, this trait of his being came to the fore; so in Arkadia and Argolis. This last landscape lacked the favor of the god, so it was called in the saga, because Inachos had assigned it to Hera and not to Poseidon, yet in one place the clear water of a spring still bubbles from the ground; it is there, where Poseidon enjoyed the love of Amymone, the daughter of Danaos.Perhaps from this trait one must also explain the large number of children, which was attributed to him (cf. *infra*).

The creation of the horse is attributed to him, the breeding of horses, riding and all related chivalric exercises were under his protection. Especially the grazing horses, the horse herds, were under the god's care, yes this even extended to all herds in general.

There are several legends about the origin of the horse. Sometimes we read that Poseidon made it appear by striking a rock with his trident, at other times it is brought forth by the earth fertilized by him. The first horse thus created was called Areion, to which, however, other legends attribute a different origin. This belonged first to Heracles, then to Adrastos.Generally, it was thought to be owed to him the taming of the horse; he had learned to lead it and to harness it. But he had to share this honor with other deities, especially with Athena, who was also considered to be the inventor of the rein, a circumstance that gave rise to a common veneration of the two deities, who were previously thought to be hostile to each other. Nevertheless, Poseidon was first and foremost entitled to the name of *Hippios*, that is, "the horse god," and to his favourites he gave beautiful horses as gifts. So the horses with which Idas succeeded in escaping Marpessa from the persecutions of Apollo, so according to some the horses, with which Pelops gained victory over Oinomaos, while other legends, on the other hand, call precisely the horses of Oinomaos a gift from Poseidon, so especially Balios and Xanthos, both horses of Achilleus. These horses, which had sprung from Poseidon, or had been given by him to his friends, were not only winged, but they also possessed the power of speech.

It goes without saying that the god, who was in such close relation to the horse, was also the god of all races, whether with horses or with horse-and-carriages. To excel in this, to have beautiful horses, to equip them in a magnificent manner for the parades held at some religious festivals, or in an expedient manner for battle, was a point of honor among the considerable and rich Greeks, especially among the Athenians. Everything connected with it was under the guardianship of Poseidon, and it seems, that in all places where the god was venerated, races were periodically held in his honor. Later two of these contests grew in stature to such an extent that they left all the others far behind, first of all that at Onchestos, in Boeotia on the shores of Lake Kopais, a town wholly and entirely dedicated to the service of Poseidon. There was a sacred forest where all the charioteers used to harness their horses, and even the fiercest and wildest horse became calm when it entered that forest. But even more magnificent than these races were the Isthmian Games, which became one of the four Panhellenic Games of the Greeks. With Poseidon, Melikertes was honored at these, and his worship peculiarly mixed some strange, alien customs among the Greek Poseidon service. The Isthmian

Games were very old. They were said to have been established by King Sisyphos of Corinth. The Corinthians governed them. The wreath given to the victors was formerly of ivy, later of pine branches, both intended to mark the sad death of Melikertes.

Amorous relationships and children

By his lawful wife Amphitrite, he had a son and three daughters, Triton, Rhode, Kymopolea and Benthesikyme.

The sons of the mighty and impetuous god are powerful and fierce creatures, so the cyclops Polyphemos by the nymph Thoosa, so the great Kyknos, who was defeated by Achilleus, so Amykos, who fell by the fist of Polydeukes, so Korynetes, Prokrustes, Kerkyon and Skiron. He hated Odysseus because he had blinded his son Polyphemus.

In no place did Poseidon enjoy reverence but people knew of women, whether of divine or human origin, who had shown their love to him there and had given him children. However, part of the reason for this is the desire to attribute divine descent to the *heros*, who was considered the progenitor of a lineage or the founder of a *polis*. Thus Poseidon is mentioned as the father of Pelasgos, Hellen, Achaios, Minyas, Boiotos, Doros, Taras, Kalaurios. The island of Kalauria is said to have been named after the latter, where there was a sanctuary to Poseidon that was the center of an early amphiction.

The love of Poseidon for Arne, that is "the lamb," which bore him Boiotos, and the myth which related that the god transformed himself into a ram in order to unite himself with Theophane, to whom he had given the form of a sheep, and conceive from her the ram with the golden fleece (see Phrixos.), are examples of the close relationship in which the god was thought to be related to these animals.

When Poseidon had conceived love for Tyro, the beautiful daughter of Salmoneus, who herself loved the river god Enipeus, and the god had united himself to her under his guise, she bore him twins Pelias and Neleus, whom she abandoned amid a herd of grazing horses. The first was suckled by a mare, but both were brought up among horses and became strong heroes, who took pleasure in all chivalric exercises, spread the cultivation of his favorite animal with the service of Poseidon, Pelias in Thessaly, Neleus in Pylos, and both were highly blessed by their father. Likewise Hippothoön, the son, whom Alope, the daughter of Kerkyon, bore to Poseidon, was abandoned by her and suckled by a mare.

The saga of Melanippe, who abandoned the twins Aiolos and Boiotos, whom she gave to the god, in a cowshed, where they were suckled by a cow and guarded by a bull, alludes in some degree to Poseidon's protection of the flocks (cf. *supra*). The fates of Melanippe and her sons were a favorite subject of the tragic poets.

In a legend native to Corinth, Poseidon is the father of the winged horse Pegasus, whom he had sired to the Gorgo Medusa. When that horse was afterwards given to Bellerophon for his use, Poseidon taught him how to tame and control it.

He is also father of Chrysaor, the very strong fighter, literally: he with the golden sword.

Those he loved included Libya, Agenor, Belos, Iphimedeia, Aloeus and Molione.

According to Plato, Poseidon had five twin sons by the woman Kleito and for reinforcement built rings on a hill, three of water, two of earth, which would become the capital of Atlantis. His eldest son was Atlas, who ruled over the princes, his nine brothers. Together they ruled the island, other islands in the Atlantic Ocean, the "continent enclosing the Ocean" and territories within the Pillars of Hercules. Their descendants degraded through lust for power and sought to annex more territory to the east. The Ancient Greeks of 9600 B.C., according to Plato, managed to defeat the Atlanteans. Zeus ended the Atlantean civilization with a Flood and earthquakes, but in the process also destroyed the Athenian civilization of the Ancient Greeks. According to Plato, Solon heard this history from Egyptian priests of Saïs.

Attributes and symbols

The god was therefore brought into close relationship with the animal world. Those animals were especially sanctified to him, in whose movements it was thought to notice some resemblance to the movements of the waves of the sea. Thus they compared the waves crashing against the steep cliffs to goats, which dared to make bold jumps to get from one rocky point to another, and the other waves to crooked-horned bulls. Even several towns, which were sanctified the god, bore their names after this, so Aigai after the Greek word *aix*, which means goat, and Helike after *helix*, which is crooked-horned. In other places billy goats and grazing lambs took their place.

95

But the favorite animal of Poseidon is the horse, either because it hops like the waves of the sea, and also carries like them, or because, like the god himself, it takes pleasure in the moist meadows.

Among the animals was further sanctified to him the dolphin, his faithful companion at sea, among the trees the pine, whose branches served as prizes in the contest celebrated in his honor and whose wood is the lumber for the ships. As sacrifices, black bulls were usually slaughtered at his service, also horses, rams and wild boars.

He is usually depicted with a trident, the weapon he had received from the Cyclopes before the battle of the Titans.

In the visual arts

Now as for the depiction of Poseidon by visual art, it corresponds fairly accurately to the descriptions of the poets. His images bear much resemblance to those of Zeus. A broad torso, long drooping locks and brilliant eyes are the hallmark of both the king of heaven and the ruler of the sea. But artists gave Poseidon more angular facial features than were found on Zeus and somewhat tangled head hair. The older art depicted him clothed; in later times it became more and more common to depict him naked even with Poseidon. Usually he has his trident in his hands and is accompanied by a dolphin. He either holds it with his hand or puts his foot on it. He is often depicted riding a bull, on a horse or in a chariot, often surrounded by all kinds of sea creatures. Sometimes he sits on a throne, other times he is depicted standing - and this is especially the case with the colossal statues of this god, which are often found near harbors and on promontories. These colossal images can also be divided into two types: first, those which depicted him with raised trident and designated him as the god of the stormy sea and earthquakes and, on the other hand, those images in which he, supporting one leg on a rock, stares into the distance on the prow of a ship or on a dolphin, giving the impression of the god who, with self-confident power, governs the sea, directs the ship and leads it into a safe harbor.

The National Archaeological Museum of Athens houses the ancient, 2.09-meter-high bronze statue of the "god from the sea," often called the "Poseidon of Cape Artemision" (found at the northern tip of Euboea). Meanwhile, some art historians believe it is more likely to be a statue of Zeus, carrying a lightning bundle horizontally in the empty, raised hand, since Zeus was the only god who had this attribute. Indeed, Poseidon did not hold his trident horizontally in the ancient representation. A comparison with the faces of other sculptures of the severe style of the 5th century BCE supports this contention.

Zeus

King of the gods and ruler of Mount Olympus | Sky deity

The Romans identified their chief god, Jupiter, with Zeus.

Zeus (common pronunciation in the Netherlands: *Zuis* or *Zeus*; Ancient Greek: Ζεύς (*Ancient Greek pronunciation:* Zdews), genitivus Διός or Ζηνός) is a figure in Greek mythology.

He is the chief god, who ruled from Mount Olympus. He was a son of Kronos (Lat. Saturn) and Rheia, two of the twelve Titans, the powerful sons and daughters of Ouranos, the sky god. Kronos was the successor of Ouranos. The equivalent of Zeus in Roman religion is Jupiter.

Eleuthereus appears to some writers as a nickname of Zeus.

The meaning of his name (Indo-European *Djev = radiant, related to Latin *dies* = day) indicates an affinity with the worship of the bright firmament; Zeus' most essential function is that of sky god. Nature and all its phenomena were subject to him. He hurled the lightning, gathered the clouds and drove them apart; rain and snowfall were caused by him. Therefore, all kinds of high mountains were considered his abode: the Ida in Crete, the Lycaeus in Arcadia, but the most famous is Olympus in Thessaly. The eagle (originally a symbol of lightning) was his sacred bird, the oak his sacred tree, his shield was the aegis. By using his thunderbolt to bring about lightning and thunder, as well as with a rainbow and the flight of birds, Zeus gave omens to man. In the oracle of Dodona, the priests could hear the will of Zeus by listening to the rustling of the oaks in the oak grove sacred and dedicated to Zeus.

Early on, perhaps as early as Mycenaean times (c. 1600 to c. 1100 B.C.), he became the central figure of the Greek pantheon and put the other gods in the background. Following the example of heads of considerable lineages on earth, they presented Zeus as the head of the family of gods. His family also had its abode on Olympus and obeyed him. Thus Zeus became not only the confirmer of harmony in nature, but above all of social order. Kings and princes derived their power from Zeus and were answerable to him. He was the consultative god, protector of the public assembly and enforcer of oaths. The family was also under his care: as Zeus Herkeios (= Protector of the court), he had an altar in the courtyard of the home. Especially guests and strangers were under his protection.

Battle of Zeus and Kronos

Zeus was the only son to escape Kronos' voraciousness, which was aroused when Gaia predicted that one of his sons would one day overthrow him from the throne. To prevent this, he swallowed all his children. But the sad Rheia managed to keep Zeus' birth a secret and she hid him in a remote, dark cave on Crete where he was raised by the nymphs. There he drank milk from the goat Amalthea and the bees brought him honey. Ida and Adrasteia, daughters of Melissa, cared for him, and the priests of that region, the Kourets, also helped protect the young god. They guarded the cave and when he cried they would beat their armor loudly so that Kronos would not hear.

When Zeus, as a grown man, confronted his father with his existence and demanded that he give back his devoured but immortal children, a tough battle for power ignited. It was between Zeus on the one hand and Kronos with most of the Titans on the other. Zeus freed the Cyclopes and the hundred-armed giants, the Hekatoncheirs, from Kronos' prison in the Tartarus and thus secured their help. He hurled his main weapon, the lightning bolts made by the Cyclopes, down from Olympus and continued to do so until he was victorious. Thus Zeus obtained dominion over the world. The brothers and sisters of Zeus swallowed by Kronos (Poseidon, Hades, Hera, Hestia and Demeter) were freed from him. A new generation of gods, that of the Olympian gods, thus came to power.

Zeus and the Giants

A second terrible struggle for power ignited when primordial mother Gaia of Earth could no longer watch some of her children being held captive in the underworld; Zeus had not released them because they had been hostile to him. She encouraged the Giants to fight the battle for heavenly dominion for her with him. Then these giants broke free from the underworld with great violence and moved furiously and excitedly toward the mountains of Thessaly.

Iris summoned all the heavens and even called for the help of the spirits of those who had died. All the elements were shaken: the heavens thundered and the earth trembled. Each god took part in the battle in his own way: Phoibos Apollo fired arrows, Hephaistos hurled glowing coals at the monsters, Poseidon fought with his trident, the Moirs (goddesses of doom) swung clubs, Heracles (Hercules) fought bravely, and Zeus himself hurled his scorching lightning bolts down again. And in the end, although the giants in their rage wrenched whole mountains loose and piled on top of each other, Zeus won the battle and became ruler of the universe forever and unchallenged, as Supreme in the circle of the gods.

Hera and other loved ones

Zeus' wife was his sister, the goddess Hera, the third daughter of Kronos. However, to her great anger and sorrow, Zeus was often struck by the arrows of the god of eternal love Eros and could not resist the love of other women. Hera was very jealous and tried in many ways to dissuade Zeus from his amorous escapades, but often in vain: he had at least nine relationships with goddesses and fourteen with mortal women from among men. He fathered dozens of children with them. He even seduced the lovely Europa by turning himself into a bull and then kidnapping it.

Nor was male love shunned in Greek mythology. Zeus, for example, had his eye on Ganymede. The story has often been discussed in terms of the role of homosexuality in Greek culture.

Sons and daughters

Together with Hera, he had Ares, the god of war. Zeus' daughter, the goddess of love and beauty Aphrodite, rose from the foam of the sea. But Aphrodite is also often seen as the daughter of Ouranos, whose genitals were taken from him by his own son and fell into the sea, from which Aphrodite arose. Hera bestowed upon him Hephaistos, the god of forging, who was able to tame the power of fire. With Leto, a daughter of the Titan Koios, Zeus had two children: Apollo, the god of prosperity and order, protector of law and of all that is good and beautiful in nature and among men, and Artemis, a protective and salvific goddess of nature. Both were unmarried. Zeus' son Heracles was born on earth. By Leda, he fathered the twins Castor and Pollux and their sister Helena, who played a major role in the Trojan War. The mortal Tantalos, king of Lydia, was also (probably) a son of his.

Finally, there was Pallas Athene, Zeus' favorite daughter, the goddess of wisdom, for she, having swallowed the goddess Metis, had sprung from his mind. She was therefore a powerful and wise leader and patron of states and cities in war and peace. Dionysos was also the son of Zeus. Dionysos was born from the hip of Zeus. Dionysos is the god of wine and relaxation. By the mortal Danaë, he fathered Perseus. The latter later became famous for his fight with Medusa, in which he beheaded her.

The goddess Iris was the messenger, through whom communication between gods and humans was conducted. Hermes was also messenger of the gods. He escorted the spirits of dead people to Hades.

Art and props

In visual art, Zeus is usually depicted as a dignified and regal man with lush beard and hair. In older representations he wears a wreath of oak leaves, later a laurel wreath. Among his attributes, depending on the function in which he is depicted, are a scepter, a sacrificial bowl, an eagle or a small Nikè, a lightning bolt and a globe.

The most famous statue of Zeus in ancient times was the seated statue made of gold and ivory (considered one of the seven wonders of the ancient world, known from some coins and by a description by Pausanias; lost) that Phidias made for his temple at Olympia.

Zeus among non-Greek peoples

In ancient times, there were many contacts between the various seafaring peoples, and they adopted many elements of the various religions from each other.

Thus, even before Hellenistic times, Zeus was known to the Phrygians and was identified as the supreme god with the god Amon, and was therefore worshiped as Zeus-Amon. Amon was considered a god among both the Egyptians and the Libyan peoples, with different interpretations.

The Romans identified Zeus with Jupiter, the Germanic peoples identified him with Wodan and the Scandinavian peoples with Odin.

Titans and Titanesses

Cronus

Cronus was later identified with the Roman god Saturn.

Kronos (Ancient Greek: Κρόνος) or **Cronus** (Latinized) is a figure from Greek mythology. The equivalent in Roman mythology is Saturn. He is the youngest of the Titans, son of Ouranos and Gaia. Cronos is often confused with the primordial god Chronos, who emerged from Chaos, but they are two separate and distinct entities similar only in name.

World domination

Kronos' father Ouranos, jealous of all his sons, threw them back into the depths of the earth. Kronos' mother Gaia wanted revenge and urged Kronos to castrate his father. This Kronos did with a sickle. He then became ruler in his father's place. He married his sister Rhea, but he did not want any of the children born of this marriage to live, for his parents had prophesied to him that one of these children would deprive him of his rule. As soon as the children were born, he devoured them with skin and hair. Thus he swallowed successively Hestia, Demeter, Hera, Hades and Poseidon. When Rheia was pregnant by Zeus, she fled to Crete and gave birth there in secret. To deceive Kronos, she gave him a stone wrapped in cloth, which was swallowed by Kronos. Thus Zeus was spared. Once Zeus grew up, he forced Kronos to ingest a mixture of wine and mustard and spit out all the children swallowed by him. With the help of his brothers, sisters, some Titans and other allies among the gods, Zeus overwhelmed and dethroned Kronos and became the king of gods and men. Together with his brothers Hades and Poseidon, he cut Kronos into pieces and threw him into the Tartaros.

Kronos and his supporters were imprisoned in the depths of Tartaros, surrounded by a three/two night, and strictly guarded by the Cyclopes and Hekatoncheirs. According to some sources, they were later pardoned and allowed to stay in the Elysian fields. Other myths say that Zeus allowed Kronos to escape to Italy, whereupon he became the ruler of Italy.

Baal Hammon

The chief god Baal Hammon of the Carthaginians was identified with Kronos in the Interpretatio Graeca.

Gaea

Gaea, or Ge, is the personification of Earth as a goddess

Gaia (Ancient Greek: Γαῖα, Γαῖη or Γῆ) or **Gaea** (Latinized) is a figure from Greek mythology. She is the primordial mother, the Earth, which arose from the Chaos at the beginning of things. Chaos contained all the basic constituents, the four elements earth, water, air and fire. From these, among other things, Gaia arose.

External Characteristics

Gaia, the goddess of nature and the Earth, was depicted as a plump woman, often rising from the ground, always attached to it. The Earth itself was seen in Greek mythology as a flat disk (flat Earth), surrounded by the river Okeanos (the ocean), supporting the sky dome of Ouranos.

Offspring

106

According to the Greek sagas and myths, Eros caused Gaia to unite with the water and the sky, thus giving birth to the sea (Pontos) and the sky (Ouranos). Also, the Titans, the three one-eyed Cyclopes and the three hundred-armed giants came forth from primordial mother Earth. The latter were called Briareos, Gyes and Kottos and each also had fifty heads. They were also called the Hekatoncheirs. The Titans and the Cyclopes were fathered by Ouranos.

As shown in the family tree, Gaia is the mother of some species. The titans and the cyclopes. There is also another species that people are not sure if it is descended from her. Namely, it is about the giants.

Gaia's motherly love plays a major role in the stories. When Ouranos felt threatened by the giant Cyclopes and imprisoned them in the abyss Tartaros, she tried to protect her children from him. She asked the Titans to help her, but only the youngest, Kronos, answered her call. Gaia gave birth to the iron in her earthly womb, made a sharp scythe and gave it to Kronos as a weapon. With it, he maimed his father Ouranos and took dominion from him. This brought crime and violence into the world.

This act of violence had further consequences, for from the drops of blood that fell into the earth sprang the Gigantes, a genus of giants, and the Erinyes, the hideous goddesses of vengeance. Moreover, an oracle was pronounced on Kronos that one of his own sons would also depose him from his throne. His son Zeus would indeed carry out the oracle.

Gaia later played another important role in the second great war for celestial supremacy, between Zeus and his opponents, the monstrous Giants. She could not stand to see her children tormented in Tartarus and called on them to fight Zeus. This they did, but without success. Zeus had become the great ruler of heaven forever after this war.

In other religions

The idea of a nature goddess is much older than Greek civilization. However, it is not known what older peoples named her. Archaeologists have found so-called Venus figurines from the Stone Age. Even today, she is revered by pagan religions, either as a goddess or as a force of nature.

Atlas

The Titan god who bore the sky aloft

Atlas (Ancient Greek: Ἄτλας - " the bearer ", from τλάω / tláô, " carry, support ") is a figure from Greek mythology. According to legend, Atlas carries the heavens on his shoulders as punishment and is associated with the Atlas Mountains, Atlantis and the Atlantic Ocean. In reality, he may have been king of Mauretania.

Gods family

Atlas is said to be the son of Iapetus, Poseidon or Ouranos. Atlas is the father of Maia and thus the grandfather of Hermes. The other six Pleiades are also daughters of Atlas and together they are called "Atlantides" ("ides" is a Greek suffix; it means son or daughter) . Calypso, who resided on the island of Ogygia, in the middle of the ocean, was also a daughter of Atlas.

Punishment

Atlas was one of the children of the Titan Iapetus. Unlike his brothers Prometheus and Epimetheus, Atlas fought on the side of the Titans who supported Kronos in the war against Zeus. Because of Kronos' advanced age, it was Atlas who led the Titans in battle. Because of this, Atlas received a special punishment from Zeus and was condemned to stand on the western edge of the earth (Gaia) and carry the celestial vault (Uranus) on his shoulders, preventing them from sustaining their original union.

Atlantis

According to Plato, Atlas was the eldest son of the sea god Poseidon and the woman Cleito and had nine brothers over whom he ruled as king. All ten had a part of Atlantis to rule over, associated islands and territories of the western continent and to the east within the Pillars of Hercules (current name: Rock of Gibraltar). The Atlantic Ocean was named after Atlantis. Their distant descendants degraded and wanted to conquer more territory in the east out of lust for power. The ancient Greeks of Athens managed to prevent that, according to Plato, about 9600 BC. Zeus ended the Atlantic civilization with a Flood and earthquakes, but at the same time ancient Greek civilization went down with it.

According to the Phoenician historian Sanchuniathon, Atlas, by order of his brother Cronus, was buried in a deep hole in the earth because Cronus did not trust Atlas. Both Cronus and Atlas, according to Sanchuniathon's history, were sons of Ouranos.

Meeting with Heracles

Atlas plays a role in the twelve works of Heracles. Heracles was instructed to steal the golden apples from the tree in the garden of the Hesperides, but a mortal could not do so with impunity, for the tree was a wedding gift from Gaia to Zeus and Hera. Therefore, Heracles went to Atlas, who according to some sources is the father of the Hesperides, and asked if he would pluck the apples while he would take the heavens from him for a while. But when Atlas returned with the apples, he did not want to take over the celestial vault again and suggested that he deliver the apples himself. Heracles used a ruse and asked if Atlas would take over the burden for a moment so that he could put a cloth on his shoulders to make the weight more bearable. When Atlas lifted the sky again for a moment, Heracles walked away with the apples.

In an alternate version, Heracles built the Herakles pillars that carry the sky, freeing Atlas from his punishment.

Origin of the Atlas Mountains

109

By Herodotos, Atlas was already equated with the Atlas Mountains of the same name. According to this myth, Atlas tried to chase away the lost Perseus. But Perseus used Medusa's head to turn Atlas into stone, and when he fell down, the Atlas Mountains were created. This story cannot be reconciled with the stories in which Atlas meets and helped Heracles with his twelve works, because Heracles is employed by Perseus' grandson, Eurystheus.

Cultural influence

Atlas is also depicted on the Palace on Dam Square in Amsterdam. Standing on the pediment on the rear facade on the Nieuwezijds Voorburgwal, Atlas towers the celestial vault. Designed by Artus Quellinus and cast by the famous bell-founder François Hemony There is also a statue of Atlas placed in the Citizens' Hall, on the western side. Children used to be told that Amsterdam would fall if Atlas dropped his globe.

Furthermore, Atlas is found between two Fama on a lot of Frisian tail clocks.

Prometheus

Prometheus (Ancient Greek Προμηθεύς) is a figure in Greek mythology, which classifies him among the genus of the Titans and sees him as the protector or even creator of man. His myths are best known from the works of Hesiodos and from the tragedy *Prometheus enthralled*, but also from later writings of pseudo-Apollodoros and Ovid. His name is said to mean "knowing beforehand" or "foreseeing," unlike his brother Epimetheus ("he who thinks afterward").

Myths

According to Hesiodos' *Theogonia of* the 8th century BCE, Prometheus was the son of the Titan Iapetos and the Oceanid Klymene (or Asia), who also later became his mistress. Other sources list Themis as his mother. Furthermore, he was the brother of Atlas and Epimetheus, among others, who married Pandora. Prometheus owed his immortality to Cheiron the centaur.

The *Bibliotheka* of pseudo-Apollodoros and Ovid's *Metamorphoses* tell that Prometheus and the goddess Athena together in the city of Panopeus created the first humans from clay. In ancient times, the sand-colored stones near this city were a tourist attraction, told to be remnants of an earlier creation experiment by Prometheus. The creation was commissioned by Zeus, who, however, was later less fond of humanity.

During a dispute between Zeus and humans over the distribution of sacrificial animals, Prometheus cast himself as arbitrator. He covered a pile of bones with tasty-looking fat, hid the best meat under a pile of entrails and then let Zeus choose first. The all-knowing deity pretended to be fooled and chose the first pile. In revenge, he resolved to withhold from man the secret of fire.

In the allocation of gifts and skills, however, humans were already disadvantaged. Both in terms of survival instincts and natural defenses, other living beings were much better off. Out of love for humanity, Prometheus stole fire from the Olympian gods and gave it to humans. He taught man to work metal with it and taught them science and art. Prometheus was represented as a teacher and inventor, who taught people mutual respect and taught them to think ahead. According to the Attic tragedy *Prometheus enthralled* - probably wrongly attributed to Aischylos - the Titan also foiled a plan by Zeus to destroy mankind.

Zeus punished Prometheus and the humans for the theft of the forbidden fire from heaven. The nemesis, the "avenging justice," fell to the Titan: he was chained to a column in the mountain range Caucasus and every day the eagle Ethon came to pick out his liver and eat it. At night the liver grew back, so the torment could begin again. The nemesis intended as eternal came to an end because the hero Heracles, with the approval of Zeus, killed the eagle during his eleventh work. Hesiodos does not mention it, but according to *Prometheus handcuffed*, the captive was also freed from his chains.

The punishment for humanity was also harsh and was not shortened. Zeus had the first woman made, Pandora and sent her with her beauty, charms and wiles to Epimetheus. This dim-witted Titan had been warned by his brother Prometheus not to accept gifts from the gods, but Pandora he accepted. She opened the jar she carried and let war, disease, poverty and other evils escape into the world. Only hope remained at the bottom.

Prometheus had a son Deukalion. The mother was Pronoia or Hesione, in each case a daughter of Okeanos. Deukalion married Pyrrha, the daughter of Epimetheus and Pandora. When Zeus sent a flood to destroy humanity, Prometheus revealed the plan to Deukalion and Pyrrha so that they could save themselves in a coffin. Prometheus here actually assumed the role of Enki in the Flood epic from Sumerian mythology. Deukalion and Pyrrha landed on the Parnassos after nine days and brought forth a new race of humans.

Sky deities

Phaëthon

Phaëton (Ancient Greek: Φαέθων), also called Phaëthon, is a figure from Greek mythology. The heros Phaëton is a son of the sun god Helios and Klymene (in some lore, he was the son of Apollo and Klymene). Menops (or Merops) was his stepfather.

Myth

Helios (the Sun) used to mount the solar chariot every day. Epaphus (Apis) was the son of Io and Jupiter (Zeus). Io, as the mistress of Jupiter, had fled from Argolis to Egypt to escape the vengeance of Juno. In Egypt, Io was worshipped as Isis. Epaphus insulted Phaëton, who was the same age as him. According to Epaphus, it was a lie that Phaëton was the son of the Sun. Phaëton's greatest desire, as proof that he was indeed the son of the Sun, was to ride this chariot as well, and one day he took the opportunity. His father had told him he could ask for whatever he wanted. He put Phaëton's halo on his head. The four fire-breathing winged solar horses Pyroïs, Eoüs, Aethon and Phlegon, however, noticed that someone else was holding the reins and bolted. The solar chariot skimmed past the earth and the heat created great arid places: the deserts, Ovid writes that Libya then became desert. Mountains caught fire and "burned bare," rivers evaporated and "great cities perished with wall and all; the fire reduced countries with their peoples entirely to ashes. Ovid mentions 25 mountains, including Etna, Alps, Caucasus and the Apennines and 24 rivers by name, including the Euphrates, Ganges, Danube, Nile, Rhine and Rhone.

Before the whole earth would be on fire, the supreme god Zeus decided to intervene. He threw a thunderbolt at Phaëton after a supplication from Mother Earth, causing the latter to fall out of the chariot, plunge "like a star" (comet) down into the Eridanus and die. The solar chariot wreckage with broken fragments, toom, chariot axle, tiller tree, wheels, etc., fell to earth, the horses returned to the sun.

Lampetia, Phaëtusa and an unnamed sister, were the three daughters of Helios and Neaera (the "Heliads"), and thus half-sisters of Phaëton. After Phaëton perished, they mourned his death. Their tears congealed into amber and the sisters were turned into poplars. Cycnus, Phaëton's friend, governor of the strong fortresses of the Ligurians, changed from grief into a swan. The sun wore mourning clothes for a long time, depriving the earth of sunlight.

Uranus

The personification of the heavens or the sky | Primordial deity

Ouranos (Ancient Greek: Οὐρανός) or **Uranus** (Latinized) is a figure from Greek mythology. He is the personification of heaven. According to Hesiodos, this celestial dome hangs as high above the earth (Gaia) as the Tartaros (the deepest part of the underworld) lies below it. A bronze anvil would take ten days to fall from Ouranos to the earth's surface. Ouranos was rarely depicted as a person.

The name *Ouranos* is sometimes associated with the deity Varuna from Hinduism. Both names are said to come from an Indo-European root meaning "to cover. However, this theory is not widely held. The Roman counterpart of Ouranos is Caelus.

Origins and descendants

Ouranos is the son and husband of Gaia, the Earth. They form the oldest pair of gods and are responsible for the creation of many mythological figures, including the Cyclopes, the Titans, the Hecatoncheirs and the Oceanids. Fearing for his offspring, Ouranos exiled the Cyclopes, the Titans and the Hecatoncheirs to Tartarus. Finally, with the help of his own wife Gaia, he himself is castrated with a sickle by his son, the Titan Kronos . His genitals fall into the sea and from the seed Aphrodite is born. From the blood that splashes on the earth the Erinyes (Furies), giants and Meliae (nymphs of the ash tree) are born. From Ouranos' castration,

Kronos rules the world with his sister and wife Rheia until Kronos in turn must give way to his son Zeus.

Aeolus

Divine keeper of the winds and king of the mythical, floating island of Aiolia (Aeolia)

Aeolus (Ancient Greek: Αἴολος, *Aiolos*; Dutch, obsolete: *Eool*) is a figure from Greek and Roman mythology. He was a son of Poseidon who was appointed by Zeus as the keeper of the winds: Boreas the north wind, Notos the south wind, Euros the east wind and Zephyrus the west wind. Aeolus kept these winds locked up in a cave and could send them out when he wanted to bring wind.

Aeolus met Odysseus in the Liparian Islands. He gave this one a bag, which contained the headwinds, so that Odysseus would never suffer from headwinds. Odysseus' traveling companions were so curious, however, that they looked into the bag. The headwinds escaped, preventing Odysseus from reaching his destination yet.

Aeolus was also the deity who prevented the Greeks from setting sail for Troy (this at the insistence of Artemis) before King Agamemnon would sacrifice his daughter Iphigeneia to the goddess.

The god is also the mythical ancestor of the Aeolians.

An *aeolian process* is a term from soil science and indicates that certain layers were formed and deposited by wind. An example is loess.

Chthonic deities

Erinyes (Furies)

Goddesses of retribution

The **Erinyes** (Ancient Greek: Ἐρινύες) are figures from Greek mythology.
They are vengeance goddesses, and pursued and tormented those who
had done something wrong. The Erinyes lived in the underworld and came
to earth when a criminal needed to be punished with their vengeance. In
Latin they were called **Furiae** - or **Dirae** - (the terrible ones), and in Dutch
Furiën.The Erinyes also had the task of guarding the Tartaros. The word
"furieus" (evil, furious) derives from the Dutch name for the Erinyes, the
Furies.

Origin

The Erinyes arose from the blood of Uranus, when the latter was
emasculated by his son Kronos and the blood fell on the body of Gaia,
mother earth. Other variants tell that the Erinyes were daughters of Nyx,
the Night. The Erinyes were three women: **Alecto**, the never-ending (the
unforgiving), **Megaera**, (the disapproving) and **Tisiphone**, (the punishing).
So they represented different aspects of punishment. The Erinyes were
older than the Olympian gods, and therefore were not subordinate to the
supreme god Zeus.

Appearance

The Erinyes looked terrifying. Their hair was made up of snakes, blood
dripped from their eyes. Sometimes they were thought to have wings like
those of a bat and the body of a dog. They had burning torches and whips
with metal barbs in their hands. Tisiphone once fell in love with Cithaeron.
He found death, however, because one of the snakes on her head fatally
bit him.

Revenge

The worst thing a Greek could do in ancient times was to kill a member of
his family. Also offending a friend or a stranger was a serious offense.
According to mythology, such a criminal was pursued by the vengeance
goddesses. The vengeance goddesses used snakes, torches and whips.
The Erinyes appeared in the dreams of the pursued and there was
nowhere to hide from them. Each time the guilty person was reminded of
his guilt. Even after the death of the guilty one did not get any rest.

According to Roman mythology, the Furiae eventually drove the culprit to madness.

When the Erinyes had time to spare or just felt like it, they would go and torture criminals in the underworld.

Only when a person was cleansed of his guilt did the Erinyes cease their revenge. The Erinyes then turned into **Eumenides** (*"Benevolent"*). A criminal could free himself from the Erinyes by repenting greatly and cleansing himself of his guilt by doing good deeds.

Orestes

One famous victim of the Erinyes was Orestes, because he killed his mother Klytaimnestra. However, this was a result of his mother having previously killed his father Agamemnon in the bath. Klytaimnestra, in turn, was angry with Agamemnon because he wanted to sacrifice her daughter Iphigenia, at the behest of Artemis.

Although Orestes had been prompted to do so by the god Apollo before committing the murder, he was still pursued by the Erinyes. The goddess Athena brought this unjust case before a special divine court, the Areopagus. Prosecutors of Orestes were the Erinyes, who acted on behalf of Orestes' mother. Defending Orestes was Apollo. In the vote, Athena's vote on the jury was decisive. Orestes was acquitted; the Erinyes reconciled themselves to this verdict and became sympathetic to Orestes.

This story shows the ancient Greeks' view of man's fate. Man cannot escape the whims of the gods: he can never do good in their eyes. The same conviction is evident in the history of Oedipus. He came from a royal family, but it was cursed: deceived by the gods, he killed his father and then married his mother.

Hecate

Hekate (Ancient Greek Ἑκάτη) is a chthonic goddess of Greek mythology and religion, and was associated with magic, spirits, the moon, night, and crossroads. The Greeks did not often depict her, but described her as a goddess with three heads: one of a dog, a horse, and a snake or lion. The origin of Hecates cult is probably in Caria, Anatolia. She was especially invoked by women during the birth of their child. She was also said to have two ghost dogs with her, and her arrival was announced by the barking of a dog. Her most famous priestess was the sorceress Medea. Hekate's feast day was celebrated in Greece on Aug. 13 and Nov. 30, and in the Roman Empire on the 29th of each month.

Etymology

Hecate, according to the *Etymological Dictionary of Greek,* is probably of non-Greek origin, possibly involving association with Greek epithets of Apollo (and Artemis). These are *hékatos* ("shooting far"), *hekatebólos* ("shooting from afar") or *hekebólos* ("striking at will"). Another etymology is *hékas*, "far away. The explanation for derivatives of *hékas, hékatos* and the like are the awesome and mysterious attributes of Hecate. In addition, the etymology has been proposed of *hékaton*, 'a hundred,' partly because

Hecate demanded sacrifices of a hundred cattle, called hecatombe, or partly because Hecate ruled over spirits of people who had not been buried, forcing them to wander for a hundred years.

Origin

Originally, Hecate is probably not a Greek goddess. According to one hypothesis, her cult came from Thrace, like that of Orpheus, for example, because her cult was clearly established at Samothrace, there are similarities between Hecate and the Thracian goddess Bendis (equated with Artemis), and because there are common ground with Phrygian cults. Another hypothesis is Caria in southwestern Anatolia, where the cult was particularly strong. For example, the Carian city of Idrias was first called Hecateia, and the city of Lagina was its main cult center in Anatolia. The local Hecate, Hecate Laginitis, was strongly associated with Zeus Panamerios, presumably giving her the role of wife of the chief god and mother goddess. There was also the annual festival "of the key" (*kleidos pompé*), referring to the mysteries of the underworld.

That her origins are not Greek suggests the fact that she does not appear in the *Iliad, Odyssey* and other early epics, whereas that would be obvious with, among other things, Odysseus' descent into the underworld in the *Odyssey*, since Hecate became known as a chthonic goddess. In the process, conflicting accounts of Hecate's genealogy existed, Hesiod claimed she had no sibling, families and clans did not claim descent from her, her temples and statues were not connected to ancient legends, and finally, her role as a terrifying ruler of sorcery does not seem to be truly Greek. Moreover, her cult does not seem to have penetrated well into more remote areas such as Arcadia, where she was not associated with Artemis, Demeter Erinys and Despoina, gods who were associated with her cult elsewhere. Finally, dogs were sacrificed to her, which was unusual in Greek religion.

Cult

Throughout antiquity the image of Hecate changed, but in general she remained a goddess of protection and destruction, of fertility and death.

Development

The development of Hecate's cult is divided into three stages. In the first stage, Hecate still showed kinship with Anatolian mother goddesses, such as the Hurritic Hepa (or Hepat). She then seemed to be more connected to the sun than to the moon and occult aspects. An early source for this ancient stage is Hesiod's *Theogony*, where she is called the "most esteemed among the immortal gods" in an ode. The second stage develops the Greek image of a terrifying Hecate, where she becomes primarily the goddess of ghosts, magic and the moon. This image is evident in the Greek magical papyri. The third stage is late paganism. She was still seen as a terrifying goddess, but her moon attribute became insignificant. Instead, the focus came to be on her role as goddess of cosmic life force and virtues that nourish the soul. This image emerged under the influence of the *Chaldean oracles*, which brought back to the fore the role of mother goddess, possibly because that aspect had continued to live on in the East but not in Greece and the western Mediterranean world.

Veneration

Temples and festivities existed for Hecate. For example, the inhabitants of Carian Stratonicea had an annual festival, the Hecatesia. At least in Athens, well-to-do residents put down plates of food to the goddess at crossroads as soon as there was a new moon. A temple, the Epipyrgídia, stood on the Athenian Acropolis near the temple of Nikè. Because Hecate ruled over border areas such as thresholds, gates and intersections, statues of her were placed throughout the city outside houses or at intersections. Those statues were used locally as oracles. As sacrifices to Hecate, people mainly used dogs, black female lambs and honey. Dogs were also part of cleansing rites. People usually prayed to her before traveling. Important places of worship were Boeotia, the island of Aegina from at least the fifth century BCE, as well as Samothrace, where the cult merged with the local mysteries. That Hecate was associated with Artemis is shown by the fact that the Artemist temple of Ephesus also contained a statue of Hecate.

Nowadays, Hecate is still worshipped by some Pagan groups including certain Wicca courts. She is seen as the Crone, the ancient wise manifestation of the triple goddess. Because she is seen as the goddess of witchcraft and the moon, she is a very important goddess within wicca. She is identified with the Cailagh, who is worshiped as a goddess within Neo-Druidism.

Mythology

As a goddess, Hecate had a minor role in Greek mythology. Apollodorus gives her a role in the Gigantomachy, but there is no mention of her in earlier versions of that story. Furthermore, there are only a few minor stories to explain, for example, one of her names, such as *Angelos*. This suggests that she did not initially have the role and reputation as in later Hellenistic times. Possibly she became more famous through association with Artemis and Demeter.

The genealogy of the chthonic goddess was unclear in ancient times. Hesiod, the earliest source in which Hecate is mentioned, called her the daughter of the Titan Perses and Asteria, and mentioned that she had no brothers or sisters. Bacchylides, however, stated that she was descended from Nyx ("Night"), while Musaeus gave Zeus and Asteria as her parents. In other accounts, she is the daughter of Admetus and a Pheraean woman, and a close relative of Aeëtes and Circe of Colchis.

Iconography

Hecate was described with various attributes. On earth, she could appear with two howling, Stygian dogs announcing her arrival. She had torches around her, and in her hair she wore oak branches and snakes. Her body is sometimes represented with three heads, or with three body parts: part horse, part dog, and part lion or boar.

Minos

King of Crete | Deified mortal and hero

In Greek mythology, **Minos** (Ancient Greek: Μίνως) was the king of Crete. The Minoan civilization was named after him. It is unknown whether this king really existed, or whether his stories were based on multiple kings, for example. Thus, it is also possible that the word Minos is "ancient Cretan" for king.

According to myths, Minos was the son of Zeus and Europa. He is said to have married Pasiphaë and was father to Ariadne, Androgeus, Deukalion, Phaedra, Glaukos and Katreus, among others. He became king of Crete when King Asterion died. Minos exiled his brothers Rhadamanthys and Sarpedon, who also laid claim to the throne. Minos lived in the Palace of Knossos.He had a labyrinth built in which the Minotaur was trapped.

After his death, Minos was appointed as one of the Three Judges of the Underworld at Hades, judging incoming souls and assigning them their proper place in the underworld. In this role, he also appears in Dante's Divine Comedy.

Persephone

The Romans called Persephone Proserpina.

Persephone (Ancient Greek: Περσεφόνεια, *Persephoneia* (especially with Homer) or Περσεφόνη, *Persephonè*; Latin: *Proserpina*) (pronunciation: "pèrseefoonee") is in Greek mythology the goddess of the kingdom of the dead and of spring. She was the daughter of Demeter, the goddess of agriculture and grain, and the supreme god Zeus. The Roman variants of Demeter and Zeus are Ceres and Jupiter.

Demeter and Persephone

Demeter loved her daughter tremendously and watched over her like a mother hen. Yet Persephone was kidnapped just as she was picking flowers in the field. Hades, the god of the underworld and ruler of the dead, emerged with horse and chariot from a chasm in the womb of the earth and pulled her onto his chariot. Persephone cried out for help, but to no avail: she disappeared with him into the darkness.

Demeter plunged into deep sorrow. After searching for a long time on earth, she also went to the constellations, where she asked Helios if she had not seen her daughter. The latter replied that Helios had seen everything, and then gave the answer herself already: Persephone is in the underworld, with Hades. Demeter was utterly powerless, and in her grief over the loss she brought a barren winter to the earth and many people suffered famine.

When things got too bad, Zeus commanded his brother Hades to return Persephone to her mother. Hades agreed, but Persephone had to eat one more supper, and there she ate six pomegranate seeds. Once something is eaten in the realm of the dead, one cannot go back. For every seed she had eaten, Persephone had to return to him for a month. And so it happened that every year she was with her mother during the spring and part of the summer, the growing and flowering season, and then she went back to the underworld, to Hades. So with Persephone, spring came to earth every year, and people spoke of the Anodos of Persephone. The myth of Demeter, Hades and Persephone can thus be seen as the Greek explanation of the origin and continuation of the seasons.

Veneration

In the mysteries of Eleusis, Persephone was worshiped under the nickname Κόρη (Korè (bet. "girl")) along with Demeter. Both goddesses formed a kind of unity where Demeter was the cultivated earth, and Korè, the grain that falls into the earth, dies and brings forth new life.

The Romans revered her as Proserpina. She was also equated there with the goddess Libera.

Gigantes and Other "Giants"

Cyclopes

A tribe of one-eyed, man-eating giants

The **cyclops**, or less commonly **kykloop**, (Ancient Greek: κύκλωψ - "round eye," from: κύκλος - "circle" and ὤψ - "eye") is a figure from Greek mythology. Cyclopes are ferocious giants with only one eye. They lived together on the slopes of the volcano Etna in Sicily, far away from the civilized world. Cyclopes would live by farming, animal husbandry and had many sheep. According to Homer, they also ate children.

The first cyclopes, named Steropes, Brontes and Arges, are, according to mythology, the children of Gaia and Ouranos. They are the assistants of the god of forging Hephaistos. To them Zeus owes his lightning, Poseidon his trident and Hades his invisibility helmet (hades cap).

In Greece, on the Peloponnese, among others, around Mycenae - the city of King Agamemnon and Eurystheus, for whom Heracles had to perform works - there were enormous walls. They served as city walls and consisted of great blocks of clay stone. These walls were so large and imposing that the Greeks believed they were not built by humans but by the Cyclopes. That is why we call them "Cyclopean walls" (see "...Cyclopea saxa," Aen. I, v.201, Verg.).

The Cyclops Polyphemos

In Homer's *Odyssey,* the hero Odysseus, in one of his wanderings, ends up on the island of cyclopes. He is captured with 12 of his men in the cave of the cyclops Polyphemos, a son of Poseidon. Polyphemos likes something other than a leg of mutton. Every night and morning Polyphemos eats two of Odysseus' men; so Odysseus devises a ruse.

Odysseus gets the giant drunk, and when the cyclops asks him what Odysseus' name is, he answers "No one. When Polyphemos falls asleep dazed from the wine and food, the men poke out Polyphemos' eye with a burning, pointed stake.

Furious with pain, the cyclops wakes up. He calls to the other cyclopes for help. They come up to the noise and ask him what is going on. Polyphemos replies, "No one put out my eye and No one escaped. I am mad at No One! The cyclopes think Polyphemos has gone mad and go back to sleep. The next morning, Polyphemos cannot find the men by touch among the sheep. He stands at the entrance to the cave knowing that his sheep are going to pasture. To escape anyway, Odysseus binds his men among sheep. He as the only one left cannot tie himself but holds on to the hair of the largest ram. When the sheep leave the cave in the morning, Polyphemos talks to his favorite ram, not knowing that Odysseus is holding on under its belly. Odysseus and his men thus manage to escape and also steal the giant's fat sheep.

Later, when Polyphemos notices that the men are no longer in the cave, he ignites a rage.

As the men row away, Odysseus calls after the giant. The enraged Polyphemos throws a rock at the ship. Even then Odysseus does not keep quiet and calls his real name. A second boulder, landing behind the ship, gives it great speed, away from the island. The hurt Polyphemos prays to his father Poseidon to avenge him. Poseidon would antagonize Odysseus throughout the rest of his long journey where he could.

Origin of the myth

One theory is that the Greeks found elephant skulls and mistook them for the skulls of giants with one large eye in the forehead. This theory was first mentioned by Othenio Abel in 1914. It is no coincidence, then, that the legend of the Cyclopes is associated with Sicily. This is where the Sicilian dwarf elephant lived during the last ice age, the Pleistocene. Elephant skulls do not have clearly identifiable eye sockets. However, they do have a large nasal cavity at the site of the trunk.

133

Adrienne Mayor further substantiates it thus in her book *The First Fossil Hunters: Paleontology in Greek and Roman Times*: The Greeks found those ancient bones and preserved them in their temples. They tried to reconstruct the appearance of the prehistoric creatures, and sought explanations for their extinction. For the latter, they relied mostly on their imagination, and that led to the mythical tales of fabulous beasts like the cyclops.

Typhon

A monstrous serpentine giant and one of the deadliest creatures in Greek mythology

Later writers identified Typhon with the Egyptian god Seth.

Typhon or **Typhoeus** (Ancient Greek Τυφάων / Typháôn or Τυφωεύς / Typhôeús, from τῦφος / tỹphos, " the burning one") was a giant, who was buried in Cilicia, in the land of the Arimoi, under the ground, which Zeus had thrown on him. He was the youngest son of Gaia, fathered to her by Tartaros, after the Titans had been overthrown by Zeus. He has a hundred fire-breathing dragon heads, with twinkling eyes and terrifying voices. He is astonishingly tall, so that he reaches from east to west with his head to the stars and with his outstretched hands. His aim is to gain dominion over gods and men, but Zeus overcomes him after a terrible battle.

By Echidna, the myth further recounted, he was the father of many hideous monsters, such as of the Chimaira, of the dog Orthros, the dragons, who guarded the Golden Apples of the Hesperides and the Golden Fleece in Colchis, of the Sphinx, of Cerberus, who guarded the

135

entrance to the underworld, of the Gorgons, of Scylla, the serpent of Lerna, the Nemean lion and the eagle Ethon, who gnawed off the liver of Prometheus. Also all the pernicious storm winds are said to have sprung from him. His dwelling place was set in various regions, which excelled because of their volcanic nature.

When Typhon and Echidna tried to attack Olympus, Zeus locked him up under Mount Etna as punishment. His wife and children retained their freedom to serve as a challenge to heroes like Heracles.

According to later sagas, the gods could not withstand his attack. They fled to Egypt and partly they hid there, partly they transformed themselves into animals. Only Zeus dared to engage in a duel with *Typhoeus* and tried to fight him with his lightning and with a harpoon, but Zeus too was vanquished.

There is a close relationship between this myth and the Hittite myth of the storm god Teshub battling the dragon Illuyankas. Representations in Greek art also show a kinship with the Hittite depiction of this battle, which was found in Malatya, Turkey.

Identification with Egyptian deities

Typhon was identified with Tabh or Seth in the Greek rendering of the Egyptian gods.

Rustic deities

Aristaeus

Minor god, protector, and creator of various arts | Defied mortal

Aristaios (Ancient Greek: Ἀρισταῖος) or **Aristaeus** (Latin) is a figure from Greek mythology. Aristaios is a satyr and son of Apollo and the nymph Kyrene.

His most famous appearance is perhaps in the myth of Orpheus, in which he stalks and chases the most beautiful water nymph Eurydice, with the result that in her flight she steps on a snake that inflicts a fatal bite on her. At this, the other nymphs take revenge. They punish Aristaios, who was a beekeeper, by killing all his bees. Aristaios could not explain why his bees suddenly died, and his mother suggested he consult Proteus. Here Aristaios learns that it is a punishment for his attempted assault on the nymph Eurydice. As penance, he will have to sacrifice four cows, four bulls, a calf and flowers to the manes of Eurydice. Nine days after the sacrifice, new swarms of bees grew from the carcasses of those cattle.

Pan

The god of the wild, hunting and companion of the nymphs

The Roman gods Faunus and Silvanus share many attributes of Pan and may have evolved from him. Some Christian depictions of the devil bear a striking resemblance to Pan.

Pan (Ancient Greek: Πᾶν) or **Faunus** (Latin) is a figure from Greek mythology. He is a son of Hermes and the nymph Penelope. Pan is the god of the wilderness and patron of shepherds and their livestock and animal instincts. Pan has the lower body and horns of a goat, but a human upper body. He also has a long narrow face, a large nose and yellow eyes.

The pan flute is named after him. He was given it when he chased the nymph Syrinx. She wanted to remain a virgin and prayed to the gods while already feeling Pan's breath on her neck. Her prayer was answered and she turned into a reed just in time. From that, Pan then made his flute.

Pan caused many mysterious sounds in the forests, which the shepherds and their herds were afraid of, the same for people in remote places. This is the explanation of the word panic. A panic fright is a sudden, general, but unfounded fright. For this reason, it was better to keep it friendly. The prefix *pan-* (everything) is also derived from Pan, because he was seen as the personification of nature. Since the Middle Ages, his appearance was adopted to depict the devil.

In the image, Pan is associated with Eros and Aphrodite because of his sensuality. However, as far as is known, Pan never had anything to do with Aphrodite or Eros. He was the son of Hermes and got along well with Dionysos. Apollo was his musical rival. The story of King Midas, about the competition between Pan and Apollo, is particularly well known.

It began with the satyr or satyr Marsyas, who found a flute that Pallas Athena had made and then discarded, because she found her cheeks got too bulbous when she blew on it. Marsyas practiced on the flute and at one point he challenged Apollo. Apollo accepted the challenge and he won over Marsyas. As punishment, Apollo would skin him alive. Pan could not stomach it, that one of his subjects met his end like that, and he challenged Apollo second. Almost everyone thought Apollo was playing better again. Pan would suffer the same fate as Marsyas, were it not for the fact that Dionysos and King Midas liked his music better than Apollo's. Apollo became so angry that he gave King Midas donkey ears because of his foolish bad taste. It is not known what the relationship was between Pan and the other gods on Olympus.

In the time of Emperor Tiberius, a boatman named Thamus, sailing near the island of Paxi, heard a voice from nowhere telling him that the great god Pan was dead. Thamus had to tell this to the people of Palodes, today Butrint in Albania. When he got near Palodes, he called out to the shore, "The great god Pan is dead!" It resounded from the shore from many throats of lamentation, and the horrified sailors told the story all over the ancient world. Plutarchus wrote it down a century later in his book *De Defectu Oraculorum*, about the silence of the oracles. Pan is the only god of whom it is mentioned that he had died. He perished in the battle between the Titans and the gods of Olympus.The ancient nature god Faunus of Roman mythology was later equated with Pan.

Agricultural deities

Adonis

The god of permanent renewal, fertility, beauty and desire

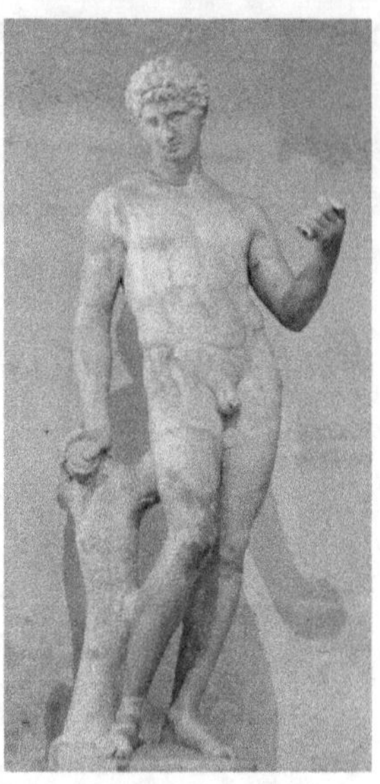

Adonis (Ancient Greek: Ἄδωνις) is a figure from Greek and Phoenician mythology. The name of this deity comes simply from the Phoenician *Adon*, meaning "lord. Like the Phoenician Adon, Adonis referred to the goddess' lover, an annual dying and resurrecting god. Adonis was the lover of Aphrodite or Venus.

Babylonia

Among the Babylonians, Tammuz was the son-lover of Ishtar. He was sacrificed annually in the guise of an innocent lamb.

Adonis comes from the Phoenician *Adon*, which, like Baal, means "lord. In fact, this was the address title of the Babylonian god Tammuz. He was worshipped especially in Byblos by the Canaanites. His cult was also transferred by Phoenician settlers to Cyprus, where his annual death and rebirth was incorporated into the cult around Aphrodite.

The bewailing of his death was the subject of the cult, long practiced in many places in the Middle East. This is also mentioned in the Bible, to the horror of the prophet Ezekiel (8.14-15). By some Israelites - especially women - the death of "*The Tammuz*" was mourned as far back as the temple in Jerusalem annually as late as 720 B.C.

An important center in the worship of Adonis was Bethlehem. Saint Jerome mentioned that in this place Tammuz (Adonis), the lover of Venus (Aphrodite or Astarte) was venerated at a sacred grove near a cave, where his death was annually mourned.

According to legend, he was raised as a shepherd boy, but was actually the son of the goddess. He was so beautiful as a baby that the goddess of the underworld didn't actually want to give him back, when he was placed in a wooden box with her for safekeeping. That didn't work out, but when Tammuz had become a youth, he was impaled on a tree by a wild boar while hunting.

Weeping, his lover, Inanna a young incarnation of the goddess, bowed over the body. She did not submit and descended into the underworld to retrieve the boy's soul. There she had to fight with Eresjkigal, her sister, but actually the dark side of herself. She got her way, in part, because every year Tammuz also had to return.

Phoenicia

In Phoenicia (Syria) and Palestine, Adonis/Tammuz was worshipped as the god of grain, which dies under the grinding stone to be baked into bread. Thus, in Bethlehem (literally "house of bread"), Adonis/Tammuz was worshiped as the god of bread. Adonis, because of his youthful beauty, was a symbol of spring and blossoming nature.

Greek mythology

According to Greek mythology, Adonis was born in present-day Lebanon from the incestuous love of the princess Myrrha and her father, Cinyras. When Cinyras discovered that he had slept with his daughter, he wanted to kill her, but the gods turned her into a myrrh tree. After nine months, the tree gave birth to a beautiful baby boy, Adonis. The goddesses Persephone and Aphrodite (she was in love with him) raised him.

Adonis was a fearless hunter, often acting recklessly when hunting dangerous game. This caused much unrest to Aphrodite, who feared something would happen to him.

In vain she begged him to leave hunting henceforth and stay with her, where nothing could happen to him. But Adonis managed to escape her laughing and continued to seek the company of the other men who went hunting so that he could continue to devote himself to his favorite pastime.

One day Adonis was pursuing a wild boar, a pursuit that provided him with great pleasure. When he finally attacked the animal, however, it suddenly turned furiously and pierced Adonis' unprotected thigh with its fearsome tusk. He still tried to get away, but his leg refused to cooperate and in this way the boar had a chance to kick him to death.

Immediately Aphrodite came to the place where her darling had met his end so tragically. She rushed through undergrowth and thorn bushes, tearing her skin open on the sharp branches and thorns. Her blood stained the white roses she passed with a dull red hue. When she arrived at the scene of disaster, Adonis was already dead and stiffened, and her passionate caresses were no longer reciprocated by him. Aphrodite then burst into such an unstoppable flood of tears that forest and water nymphs, gods and men and even nature joined her and mourned with her for the beloved young man.

Finally, reluctantly, Hades arrived at the sad crowd to take the soul of the deceased to the underworld, where he would be welcomed by Persephone, the goddess of the underworld. She would take him to the place where good, virtuous mortals dwell in bliss for eternity, called the Elysium. Aphrodite was still inconsolable and cried many, many tears. As soon as the tears touched the ground, they turned into anemones, and the drops of blood that had flowed from Adonis' thigh and fallen to the ground grew into beautiful red roses.

Aphrodite still remained so intensely sad, however, that at one point she could bear it no longer. She went to Olympus, where she fell down at the feet of Zeus and begged him to release Adonis from death's embrace, or allow her to share his fate in the underworld.

It was impossible to allow the goddess of beauty to leave the earth and go to the underworld, but Zeus could not stand to hear her pleading like this either. He therefore decided that Adonis would be recalled from the underworld so that Aphrodite could have him with her again. But Hades had control over Adonis, for the underworld was his realm and he refused to let him go. After a lengthy discussion between Zeus and Hades, a settlement was reached. Adonis was allowed to spend one half of the year on earth and had to return to Elysium for the other half.

At the beginning of spring, Adonis left the underworld and as soon as he could he went to his beloved Aphrodite. Everywhere he set his footsteps, flowers sprouted and birds began to chirp to show how happy they were at his arrival. Thus Adonis became the symbol of vegetation, rising from the soil every spring and covering the earth with beautiful leaves and flowers and causing the birds to chirp. In autumn, Adonis reluctantly returned to the underworld, for then the cruel wild boar of winter came again to pierce him with his fang and wither nature. And every year in autumn, nature wept for his departure.

Symbolism

The story of Adonis belongs to the tradition of peace offerings, similar to the story of Easter.

Nowadays, adonis refers to a beautiful boy or a handsome muscular man, as seen, for example, in the Greek statues from the time of the first Olympic Games.

In Ovid's Metamorphoses, Adonis is killed by a wild boar while hunting, after which he turns into an anemone. That flower offers only brief joy because its light weight makes it fragile and vulnerable and it is often snapped by the wind.

Every year at the beginning of spring, in the East and in Rome, the Feast of Adonis was celebrated; according to Ovid because Venus wanted his death to be relived and displayed, an afterglow of her lamentation.

Health deities

Aesculapius (Asclepius)

The god of medicine

Asklepios (Ancient Greek: Ασκληπιός, *Asklepios*; Latin: *Aesculapius*; Dutch *Asclepius*) is the god of medicine and healing in Greek mythology.

Background

He was the son of Apollo and Coronis. However, the pregnant Coronis fell in love with the mortal Ischys. Apollo killed his unfaithful lover and transformed (according to Ovid) the white raven that had delivered the news into a black one. He extracted the child from the dead mother's body and Asklepios came into the world in Epidaurus. Asklepios was entrusted by Apollo to the wise centaur Chiron, who taught him medicine. Asklepios proved so talented, however, that he was able to raise the dead to life, an ability he is said to have used several times (including on Theseus' son Hippolytus). Zeus, however, felt that raising the dead was a violation of order, and he killed Asklepios with his lightning. Apollo, however, retaliated by killing the Cyclopes (the makers of Zeus' lightning bolts). Apollo was punished and had to spend one year in the service of a mortal, Admetus, but he was successful as Zeus called Asklepios back to life.

With Homer, he is not yet a god, but a skilled physician; only from the 5th century B.C. onward is he revered as the god of medicine.

The three daughters of Asklepios were Hygieia (goddess of health), Achelois (goddess of the moon and pain relief) and Panacea (goddess of medicines). He is also said to have had two sons, the skilled physicians

Podalirius and Machaon (mentioned by Homer in the Iliad). The famous physician Hippokrates is also considered a descendant of Asklepios.

Exactly what the truth is is uncertain. Whether Asklepios actually worked at Epidaurus is something of lore. There was certainly a spa at Epidaurus and probably one of the first organized hospitals known to exist. Legend has it that people went to Epidaurus when they were sick. When one saw a snake in a dream, one was cured (see also the Asklepios cult in Epidaurus). Thus Asklepios is usually depicted with a staff with a snake winding around it, the Asklepios staff or esculape. It has been the symbol for physicians for centuries. This symbol is also used for pharmacists, with a bowl at the top of the asklepios staff, from which the snake is fed. This bowl is the symbol of Hygieia, the goddess of health and daughter of Asklepios.

Veneration

The sanctuary of Asklepios is characterized by a temple under which a labyrinth was built, in which snakes were kept.

In several places in Greece there are remains of sanctuaries dedicated to Asklepios, such as the Asklepieion on the Greek island of Kos, as well as in Epidaurus and Trikala, and in Pergamon (Asia Minor).

Other deities

Charites (The Graces)

Goddesses of fertility, charm, and beauty

The (three) **Graces** (Latin: *Gratiae*), **Charites** (Greek: *Charites*) or the **trite of the Afflictions**, were three sisters from Greek and Roman mythology.

According to Greek mythology, they were the daughters of Zeus and Eurynome but in some stories they are also the offspring of Dionysus and Aphrodite (Venus), or of Helios and the naiad Aegle. According to Roman mythology, they were the daughters of Bacchus and Venus.

The Graces are:

- Aglaia, she represents beauty and brilliance.
- Euphrosyne, she represents joy.
- Thalia (or Cleta), she represents (blossoming) happiness.

Peitho (according to the Romans, Suada) is sometimes named fourth. Together they represent fertility, creativity and charm.

The Graces were often associated with the nine muses. The river Cephissus near Delphi was dedicated to them.

Graces in art

The Graces inspire human talent and creativity and are themselves a favorite subject in art. They are usually depicted as standing with the three of them facing each other with their arms over each other's shoulders.

They are also often depicted in the Elysian Fields, the celestial underworld of the Greeks.

Mortals - Defied mortals

Achilles

Achilles (Latin) or **Achilleus** (Ancient Greek: Ἀχιλλεύς, *Akhilleús*) is a figure from Greek mythology. He is the main hero of the Trojan War and the main character in Homer's book, *Iliad*. Homer describes the hero as the cleanest, bravest, strongest and loftiest of all heroes. Later legends (Statius) describe that Achilles was only vulnerable in his heel. Consequently, this became his death; he died from a poisonous arrow hitting him in his heel. The term Achilles' heel can be traced to this story.

Achilles was the son of Peleus, the king of the Myrmidons in Greek Thessaly, and the Nereid Thetis, the daughter of Nereus, the grandson of Aiakos (Aeacus) and therefore a descendant of Zeus. He is often called "Peleide" or "Aiakide," *epithets* recalling the lineage of the swift-footed Achilles. Together with Deidameia, daughter of King Lykomedes of Skyros, he had a son Neoptolemos, also a distinguished hero of the Trojan War.

Life

He was the bravest, cleanest, strongest and loftiest of all the Greek heroes who went to Troy, and the greatest figure in the *Iliad* of Homer, who in this epic poem has sung the praises of his deeds, without, however, telling anything of his life before the march. This life, according to later writers,

153

was very rich in miraculous events. He also killed many people, including in the war against Troy. Central to the myth of Achilles is his relationship with Patroclus, described in various sources as deep friendship or love. He was killed in the battle against Troy.

Character

Achilles has a complex character. He emerges in the *Iliad* as an ideal, young, beautiful, brave and fighting hero with strong emotional traits. For example, he has a strong hatred for enemies and a great love for his friends, is easily moved to tears and acts hastily. Achilles makes decisions from the emotions he feels. More and more emphasis has been placed on this emotional side over the years. He was later considered the antithesis of the stoa, where the emphasis is placed on reason rather than feeling. Odysseus is a good example for this philosophy, acting from his mind.

What is remarkable about Achilles is that despite his extreme expressions, he possesses insight and self-knowledge. Unlike Hektor, he already knows that he will die. In his speech (Iliad IX, 308-429), he doubts his duty as a hero and considers returning home. Rather, he would rather live a quiet life at home than gain honor in the Trojan War. Because he is aware of his mortality (his beloved Patroclus is dead and he himself will die), he finishes off his enemies in cold blood without mercy.(Iliad XXI, 34-135)

Birth and youth

Before their marriage, Zeus and Poseidon had also vied for the hand of the sea nymph Thetis, until Prometheus informed Zeus of a prophecy: Thetis would give birth to a son who would surpass his father. Therefore, the two gods withdrew as suitors and allowed her to marry Peleus. As with most myths, there is also an alternative version of this story: in the *Argonautica* (IV 760), Hera alludes to the chaste rejection of Zeus' advances by Thetis, who would thus have been loyal to Hera's marriage bond.

According to Statius in his *Achilleis*, the only known source for this version, Achilles' mother immersed him in the fountain of the Styx (river in Hades, the underworld) immediately after his birth to make him invulnerable. In doing so, Achilles remained vulnerable only at his heel, the spot where his mother had held him during the immersion. According to an older myth, Thetis smeared him with ambrosia and then held him over a magical fire to burn away the mortal part. When she was interrupted in this by her husband, she left him and her child in her anger.

Nevertheless, none of the sources for Statius says anything about this invulnerability. Homer even recounts in his *Iliad* how Achilles was injured: the Paeonian *heros* Asteropaeus, son of Pelegon, challenged Achilles at the river Skamander. He simultaneously threw two spears, one of which grazed Achilles' elbow, "drawing a trail of blood."

Even in the fragmentary poems of the *Epic Cycle* that contain a description of his death, such as the *Cypria* (unknown author), the *Æthiopis* by Arctinus of Miletus, the *Iliad Mikrà* by Lesche of Mytilene and *Iliou pèrsis* by Arctinus of Miletus, there is no reference to his invulnerability or his famous Achilles' heel. In the later vase paintings depicting Achilles' death, the arrow (or in many cases arrows) strikes his body.

His father gave him Phoinix for tutor, the son of Amyntor, who taught him wrestling, walking, riding and the game of the zither. He was given the horses Xanthus and Balius, which had been given to his father as wedding gifts. In addition, he received instruction in surgery on Mount Pelion from the Centaur Cheiron.

War against Troy

He set out for Troy in fifty ships, accompanied by his tutor Phoinix and his bosom friend Patroclus. Achilles had to choose between a long and peaceful but inglorious life and an early but famous death. To the sadness of his mother, he chose the latter. During the first years of the Trojan War, he destroyed twelve cities on the coast and eleven in the Trojan interior, and as long as he fought in the ranks of the Greeks, they always retained the upper hand over the Trojans. In all dangers he was under the special protection of Pallas Athena and of Hera.

When the Greeks were exporting for war against Troy, they happened to dock in Mysia, where King Telephos ruled. In the battle that then broke out, Achilles inflicted a wound on Telephos that would not heal. Telephos sought the counsel of an oracle, which declared that "he who wounds shall heal."

According to other accounts in Euripides' lost play about Telephos, he went to Aulis dressed as a beggar and there asked Achilles to heal his wound. Achilles refused and claimed to have no medical knowledge. Thereupon Telephos held Orestes hostage, for whose release he demanded Achilles help heal his wound. Odysseus then reasoned that it was the spear that had inflicted the wound and therefore the spear should also be able to heal them. Pieces of the spear were scraped off the wound and Telephos healed.

According to Plutarchus and the Byzantine scholar Ioannes Tzetzes, as soon as the Greek ships arrived in Troy, Achilles fought and killed Cycnus of Colonae, a son of Poseidon, who was invulnerable outside his head.

According to Dares Phrygius' *De excidio Troiae historia* ("Account of the Destruction of Troy"), the Latin summary that passed on the story of Achilles to medieval Europe, Achilles saw Troilus, the youngest son of Priamos and Hekabe (some say Apollo was his father), while drinking his horses outside the walls of Troy at the Fountain of Lions. Achilles was enamored by Troilus' beauty, described by Ibycus as "gold thrice refined." Troilus rejected Achilles' advances and sought refuge in the temple of Apollo. Achilles then pursued Troilus into the sanctuary and beheaded him on the altar of the god himself. At that time Troilus would have been a year under twenty, according to legend the age Troilus had to reach for Troy to become invincible.

The Briseys affair

In Lyrnessos, one of the cities he conquered, Achilles captured a beautiful girl, Briseïs, the daughter of Brises. Agamemnon, the commander-in-chief of the Greeks, had captured the beautiful Chryseïs in a similar action. She was a daughter of Chryses, a priest of Apollo. Her father offered a huge ransom for her, but Agamemnon refused to return Chryseis. As a result, plague broke out in the Greek camp at the hands of Apollo. Finally, Agamemnon was advised by Calchas, who was supported in this by Achilles, to return her to her father and make great sacrifices in honor of Apollo in order to avert the plague again. In revenge, Agamemnon claimed Briseis, to punish Achilles for supporting Calchas. Achilles was stubborn and continued to sulk because he had lost Briseis. He still refused to join the fight and only interfered again after the death of his friend Patroclus (who had put on Achilles' armor).

Death of Achilles

According to most stories, Achilles was killed by an arrow shot by Paris. Some legends thereby tell that that arrow was shot into Achilles' heel, that the arrow was poisonous or that the arrow was guided by Apollo. Nevertheless, Paris, usually depicted as a coward, does not get credit for this act in all the stories. The place varies in the myths. Sometimes it takes place on the battlefield, sometimes it happens during the marriage to Polyxena.

Veneration

The cult of Achilles was not limited to his tomb: he was also venerated in Erythrai (Asia Minor), Sparta and Elis (Peloponnese) as well as on Astypalaia, a Cycladic island. There was an archaic cult of Achilles on Leuce Island, the White Island, in the Black Sea, with a temple and an oracle that continued into the Roman period.

Ganymede

A handsome Trojan prince, abducted by Zeus and made cupbearer of the gods

Ganymede (Ancient Greek: Γανυμήδης; Latin: *Ganymede* or *Catamitus*, from which the word *catamite*, boy of shame, is derived) is a figure from Greek mythology. He was the son of King Tros, the founder of Troy, and the shepherd of his father's cattle. The gods had their eye on him because he was - as Homer says - "the most beautiful of mortals" (*Iliad* 20, 233). Homer relates that his father received a number of horses from Zeus as compensation (*Iliad* 5, 265-267). In later versions it becomes a homoerotic story and it is Zeus himself who ignited in love for the boy when he saw him grazing a flock of sheep on Mount Ida. He robbed him with the help of an eagle and in the last version even in the guise of an eagle and brought him to Olympus where the boy became a wine pourer. The latter version can be read in Ovid's *Metamorphoses* (XI, 765), which later became the most famous source for the story.

Even in the Middle Ages, Ganymede was still performed, as in *Ganymede and Helena* in which homosexuality is discussed remarkably openly for the time.

Ganymede as a motif in art

The figure of Ganymede with the eagle was often depicted in art, specially in the Renaissance and Baroque periods. The story was explained allegorically and was said to represent the desire of the human soul for union with God, with Ganymede representing the human soul and Zeus representing God. However, this allegorical explanation must often have been merely a pretext for depicting a homoerotic scene. Very different approaches can be seen with Correggio, Annibale Carracci, Gabriel Ferrier, Rubens and Rembrandt. Later artists also took up the theme, such as Thorvaldsen, Christian Wilhelm Allers and Hans von Marées.

Hercules

One of the strongest and most celebrated of the heroes of classical mythology

Hercules is the Roman name for Heracles, a figure from Greek mythology. Under the name Hercules, he was worshiped as a god in ancient Rome. According to Titus Livius, the cult of Hercules was the only one accepted by Romulus at the founding of Rome. In Armenia, it was identified with the Armenian god Vahagn (Վահագն).

Besides the usual Greek stories about Heracles that the Romans adopted, there are also Roman stories about Hercules. For example, Virgil tells in his *Aeneid* that the fire-breathing monster Cacus, who had hidden the herd of Geryones in his cave on the Aventine, was killed by Hercules. Because of this fact, Hercules himself or Euander is said to have established the cult of Hercules, at the site of the Ara Maxima on the Forum Boarium. This was an appropriate place for the worship of Hercules, since the Forum Boarium was one of the commercial centers of ancient Rome, and Hercules (like Mercury) was considered the protector of merchants. Hercules was further honored with at least twelve other shrines and temples in the city.

Heroes

Aeneas

A hero of the Trojan War and progenitor of the Roman people

Aeneas is the hero of Virgil's Aeneid but was revered by the Romans long before the Aeneid was written. They called him Jupiter indiges-"the founder of the race."

Aeneas (Ancient Greek: Αἰνείας, *Aineias*) was a mythological Trojan hero. Aeneas is the son of the goddess Aphrodite (Venus in Roman mythology) and a mortal man, Anchises, and thus can be considered a demigod. Aeneas is introduced into literature by Homer (*Iliad*, Book II) as the leader of the Dardanians (Trojans). He is the main character in the epic *The Aeneid*, by Virgil, which tells how, after his flight from Troy, Aeneas went with many wanderings to Latium (in Italy) after which his descendants will found Rome.

Aeneas in the Iliad

According to Homer (who himself built on a long literary tradition), Aeneas is a Trojan hero who, aided by Pallas Athena, takes on Diomedes (Book V). Injured by Diomedes, who threw a rock at him, he is rescued by

Aphrodite after which Apollo takes him under his wing. Diomedes attacks Aeneas three times and is cast out by the god three times. Aeneas is cared for and healed in the citadel of Troy by Leto and Artemis. Apollo creates an "Aeneas ghost" to distract Diomedes, just as later in the *Aeneid* an Aeneas ghost is created to distract Turnus. Later, Aeneas considers fighting Menelaus but when Menelaus gets help, Aeneas renounces.

In Book XX, Aeneas challenges Achilles but when Achilles injures him and is about to kill him, Aeneas is saved by the divine intervention of Poseidon who values Aeneas' reputation for piety. Poseidon exhorts Aeneas not to challenge superior fighters. Before the actual battle, Homer gives the genealogy of Aeneas with the promise that he will restore the dynasty of Priamus and Troy.

Aeneas in the Aeneid

Aeneas' father, Anchises, was of the same blood as the king of Troy, Priamus. Aeneas' wife, Creüsa, was of the same blood, only slightly further related. When the Greeks invade the city through the Horse of Troy, Aeneas, like all the other Trojans, is still asleep, but in a dream Hector comes to him and tells him to flee with his own (guardian gods of Troy) to build a new Troy somewhere else. Hector also tells him to bring the Penates (household gods) of Troy to safety; he had already brought them with him. When Aeneas wakes up, Troy is already on fire and the household gods are at his feet.

After still fighting stubbornly and against his better judgment for some time, he returns home. With his old father Anchises and the treasures on his back and with his son Ascanius/Julus by the hand, he leaves his home with Creüsa.

He had agreed with the other refugees to gather at a remote temple. Once there, however, he notices that his wife is no longer following him. He heads back, into the burning Troy, but when he arrives at his house, it is already on fire. He turns around and wants to continue his search when he suddenly hears his wife's voice and sees her figure: her spirit tells him that she has already descended into the underworld. Aeneas wants to embrace her one last time but he grabs the air. He returns to the gathering point at the temple, after which Aeneas and his companions begin their long journey.

Conversions

163

Back at the temple, the group of refugees turns out to be considerable, and the displaced Trojans, who by now have chosen Aeneas as their leader, flee the city in boats and begin their journey by sea. After a long wandering with several landings, where each time it becomes clear that the gods do not want them there, they are finally cast into North Africa by a storm.

The storm, caused by Hera (in Roman mythology:Iuno), breaks the fleet in two, after which the two groups arrive separately on the beach of Carthage. Aeneas, who manages to land with seven ships, goes exploring with his friend Achates and encounters Aphrodite (Venus), his mother, who tells them about Dido and Carthage. Aeneas and Achates are temporarily enveloped in a cloud of invisibility by the goddess and they walk toward Carthage. There Aeneas sees the other group of Trojans, led by Illioneus, pleading for help from the queen of Carthage, Dido. After a while, the cloud of Aeneas and his companions breaks apart and Aeneas' group appears before Dido. This meeting was the beginning of a time of rest for the Trojans. They lived with Dido at court for quite some time.

But Fatum (fate) had decided not to let Aeneas' journey end there and Jupiter (Zeus) informed Aeneas through Mercury, the messenger of the gods, that he should continue his journey, first to Cumae to descend to the underworld through a priestess to speak to his father. With this, Aeneas was not very happy, although he had foreseen this. On the sly, he prepared to leave. Dido, however, got wind of the matter and tried to persuade him to stay. She even wanted to hand over power to him. But Aeneas did not yield; nor could he do otherwise, for the will of the gods had to be obeyed. So the Trojans left again. Aeneas looked back once more and saw Dido standing on a hill. She cursed Aeneas and cried out that the city he would found would always remain an enemy of Carthage. Then she pierced herself with his sword.

Latium

After an auspicious voyage - the sea god Neptune thought they had had enough misfortunes at sea - they arrived in Cumae. Aeneas obtained a golden twig and, together with the priestess, descended into the Tartarus. As it turned out, his father resided in a better part of the underworld (The Elysium). Anchises told him that he already knew the future and he pointed out to his son the souls that would later reside in the bodies of Julius Caesar, Augustus and many other future Roman authority figures. He also said that a tough battle awaited Aeneas in Latium, the land he had been promised.

After visiting the underworld, the Trojans traveled to Latium. Here ruled
King Latinus, who in earlier times had heard prophecies of a strange
people who would one day come and become powerful. So he decided to
remain friendly and cleverly offered his daughter Lavinia to marry him. By
her mother Amata, Lavinia had already been promised to Turnus, the chief
of the Rutuli tribe. Incited by one of the Furies, Turnus called for a war
against the Trojans. However, Aeneas still had plenty of time to build a fort
with his men and find allies in the area. After a battle, won by the Trojans,
Turnus retreated. Later, Turnus killed the young hero Pallas, the son of
King Euander, a Latin king who was too old to fight himself but sent his
son with Aeneas. In Book XII, it finally comes to the confrontation between
Aeneas and Turnus. Aeneas did not want many innocents to die and
offered to duel with Turnus so that the war could be decided. Turnus
agreed, but Iuno sent the plan into disarray, and it came to a battle
anyway. When the battle had been going on for some time, Turnus and
Aeneas ordered their men to stop fighting so they could duel. Aeneas, who
was older, stronger and more experienced than the young Turnus, won
the duel. The epic ends in medias res: Turnus begs for his life and
promises submission, but Aeneas then sees Turnus wearing the belt of
Pallas, whereupon he kills him in anger.

Ajax the Great
A hero of the Trojan War and king of Salamis

Ajax or **Aias**, from the Latin *Aiax*, Ancient Greek: Αἴας, was in Greek mythology one of the main heroes in Homer's *Iliad*. He was a son of Telamon and is called the great Ajax, in contrast to Ajax, the son of Oileus, another hero in the Trojan War cycle, who is called the little Ajax. Together they are called the Aiants.

Life

Ajax was the son of the Argonaut Telamon, king of Salamis, and Periboia, a daughter of Alkathoös. It is said that his name was derived from the eagle, *aietos*, which his father saw when he prayed to Zeus to grant him a brave son. Ajax spoke little and slowly and had tremendous courage. He was one of Helena's suitors, who had taken an oath to help the one who became her husband. Because of this, he fought in the Trojan War, described by Homer in the Iliad. His courage and strength were out of proportion to the 12 ships, which he brought from Salamis. He was the second greatest hero of the Greeks who fought at Troy, according to the Iliad, after Achilles. He is referred to in the Iliad as enormous in stature, literally standing head and shoulders above the rest. His epithet is "bulwark of the Greeks," notable for his armor is his huge shield of oxhide. He was never wounded during all the battles in which he participated at Troy. One passage describes the impression he made on the Greeks and Trojans:

While they were thus speaking, Ajax armed himself in the fearsome
bronze. When he had fully armored himself, he went forward as the giant
Ares goes to war in the midst of men, whom Zeus has brought together in
furious battle and consuming strife. So the giant Ajax, the bulwark of the
Greeks, appeared with a smile on his grim countenance. With great strides
he advanced, brandishing his long lance. With joy the Greeks looked at
him, but a trembling fear came over the Trojans, every one's heart, yes,
even Hektor's, pounded in his chest. But it was not now possible to recoil
or creep within the throng of his men; he had challenged to battle. Ajax
approached bearing his shield, like a bulwark so large, studded with
bronze, made of seven cattle hides by Tychios, ...

Hektor, the most powerful on the side of Troy, challenged the Greeks to
decide the war among themselves with one of them. For this, Ajax was
chosen by lot by the Greeks. He fought in the duel with Hektor, almost
killing him with a large stone, but the battle was abandoned because it
was too dark. They then exchanged gifts, with Ajax giving a purple sword
belt and Hektor a sword. Ajax was a friend of Achilles, as evidenced by the
fact that he helped persuade Achilles to fight again. The next day, when
Odysseus was wounded, Ajax rescued him. When the Trojans reached
the wall protecting the ships of the Greeks, he and the other Ajax kept the
Trojans at bay. However, Ajax, despite his courageous action near the
ships, could not prevent the Trojans from setting fire to a Greek ship. The
situation was saved by Patroklos, dressed as Achilles, and the Myrmidons.
After Patroklos was killed by Hektor and stripped of his armor, Ajax
protected the corpse with his great shield. At the funeral games of
Patroklos, Ajax participated in several games, wrestling against Odysseus
and being defeated by Diomedes in spear throwing. Later, it is described
how Ajax dragged away the corpse of Achilles, keeping it out of the hands
of the Trojans while Odysseus kept the Trojans at bay.

There are several stories about the death of Ajax. The best-known story is
that of Homer in the Odyssey and after which Sophocles wrote a tragedy:
Aias. According to this story, after Achilles' death, there was a dispute
between Ajax and Odysseus over who could have Achilles' armor. The
Greek leaders would have voted on it or else they would have let the
decision be made by the captured Trojan diviner Helenos, son of Priamos.
In any case, Odysseus was given the armor. Driven by anger and
jealousy, Ajax wants to take revenge on the Greek leaders at night, but
Athens drives him insane, leading him to kill a flock of sheep instead of the
Greek leaders. Once he regained his senses, he committed suicide from
shame and remorse with the sword he had received from Hektor. Where
his blood fell on the ground, hyacinths bloomed in the letters AI, the first
two letters of his name but also, translated into Dutch, the Greek for "O

woe!" or "Alas!" It is also said that when Odysseus' ship was wrecked during all his wanderings, Achilles' armor was washed up at Ajax's grave and so, by divine justice, he still got what belonged to him.The great Ajax, according to another story, was killed by an arrow from Paris, as was Achilles, but according to yet another story, the Trojans buried him alive by throwing clay at him. They could not kill him because he had been made immortal by Heracles, who had wrapped him in his lion skin.

Ajax had a son, Eurysaces, "broadshield," who succeeded Telamon as king of Salamis. Ajax himself was never king of Salamis, but was revered there.

Daedalus

A creator of a mazelike labyrinth

Daedalus (Latin) or **Daidalos** (Greek: Δαίδαλος), son of Eupalamus and Alcippe, is a well-known figure in Greek mythology, known as an inventor, sculptor and architect. The most famous story about him is about the labyrinth on Crete and the flight with his son Ikaros.

Daedalus and Perdix

According to the Athenians, Daedalus first lived in their city.Daedalus, according to myths about him, was a highly regarded architect and the creator of lifelike statues. Several inventions were also attributed to him, such as the axe and the sail. He was considered the greatest creator of his time.

However, one of his disciples, his own nephew, was able to surpass him. That nephew - or his mother, Daedalus' sister - was named Perdix; the Greek word πέρδιξ (*perdix*) means partridge and was also chosen centuries later as the scientific name of the partridge.

In fact, the student designed the compass and while studying a fish with a spiny back, he came up with the idea of the saw. Out of jealousy, Daedalus pushed Perdix off the Acropolis of Athens, but the goddess Pallas Athena, patron of wisdom, saved the falling Perdix by turning him into a partridge, a species of bird that does not fly high, but low, out of fear because of his earlier fall.

Despite that rescue, Daedalus was accused of murder by his fellow townsmen. He accordingly fled the city of Athens and set out for Crete.

Daedalus on Crete

In Crete, Daedalus entered the service of King Minos. There he designed a dance stage for Minos' daughter Ariadne.

The vain Minos defied the gods: he exchanged a white, sacred bull he had received from Poseidon to sacrifice to that god for a gray one. The god punished Minos by beating his wife, Queen Pasiphaë, with insanity. In infatuated frenzy, she wished to experience intercourse with that bull. Daedalus was responsible for the wooden cow that allowed the queen to have intercourse with the bull. The monstrous result of that mating was the Minotaur. Daedalus was then commissioned by the king to design the Labyrinth of Knossos, where the monster was held captive.

Daedalus and Icarus

The story of Daedalus and his son Ikaros, whom he had fathered with Naucrate, is described in Ovid's *Metamorphoses*, among others.

After building the labyrinth, he and Ikaros got stuck in Crete because Minos would not let them leave, due to the fact that he knew the secret of the labyrinth of Knossos. Since Crete is an island and the ports were guarded, escape was very difficult.

Escape was only possible by air. Daedalus therefore made two pairs of enormous bird wings from feathers, which he attached to wooden frames with beeswax. Together with his foolhardy son Ikaros, he then ventured across the Aegean Sea from Crete to Athens. He advised his son not to fly too high, that is, not too close to the sun. Nor should he fly too low, since otherwise the water would wet the feathers. He had to take the Golden Middle Way or the Aurea Mediocritas.

Ikaros, however, did not listen to his father's advice. He became overconfident and flew higher and higher. The heat of the sun caused the beeswax to melt and the wings disintegrated, whereupon Ikaros plunged into the sea. Daedalus saw his son disappear into the waves. Meanwhile,

a shepherd, a fisherman and a farmer watching from a distance mistook
Daedalus and Ikaros for gods, because only gods could cleave the sky.

The grieved Daedalus buried his son after finding him on a nearby island,
traditionally the island of Ikaria. The part of the sea into which Ikaros had
ended up (between the Cyclades and Asia Minor) was named after him:
the Icarian Sea.

Jason

Jason (Ancient Greek: Ἰάσων, *Iásôn*) in Greek mythology was the son of King Aeson, king of Iolkos, a city in Thessaly. King Aeson was deprived of rule by his half-brother Pelias. When Jason was born, his parents were afraid Pelias would kill him, so they secretly sent him to the Pelion Mountains, where he was raised by the wise Centaur Cheiron.

 As a young man of twenty, Jason returned to Iolkos to claim kingship. He demanded his father's throne back and Pelias said he could have it, but he also told Jason that he was plagued by the spirit of Phrixos who demanded that the Golden Fleece be retrieved.

Jason decided to undertake the trip and gathered a large number of Greek heroes for the journey, including Heracles, Theseus, Peleus, Meleager, Laertes, Zetes and Calais, Castor and Pollux and the singer Orpheus. The participants in the expedition are called the Argonauts because their ship is called the Argo.

The journey led to Colchis on the eastern side of the Black Sea. Once there, he asked the king of Colchis (Aietes) for the Golden Fleece. The latter was willing to give it if Jason could first perform a task: Jason had to tame two fire-breathing bulls the Khalkotauroi and plow the field with them, then sow dragon's teeth and defeat the warriors who would grow up from them. With the help of Medea, the king's daughter, Jason managed to complete the tasks. However, her condition for this help was that Jason had to promise to marry her.After successfully completing this task, Jason returned to the king to receive the Golden Fleece. Aietes, surprised and angry that Jason had passed his orders, told Jason that the Golden Fleece was guarded by a dragon; to obtain it, Jason would first have to defeat the dragon. Orpheus sang the dragon to sleep, allowing Jason to take away the Golden Fleece. Aietes became no less angry that Jason had managed to get the Golden Fleece anyway, especially when daughter Medea and his young son (the heir to the throne) sailed with him. He went after the Argo with his ships. Medea knew nothing better than to dismember her little brother and throw him overboard; Aietes was left with no other option but to have his ships collect his son's pieces so he could be buried and let the Argo go.

Jason and Medea married and had children. When Jason, years later, fell in love with another woman, Medea became so angry that she killed her two children. She then toppled the Argo on Jason while he was sleeping in its shadow, killing him.

Mythology also mentions poisoning with bull's blood.

Odysseus

Some Roman writers tended to disparage Odysseus as the destroyer of Rome's mother city, Troy. Other Roman writers (such as Horace and Ovid) admired him.

Odysseus (Ancient Greek: Ὀδυσσεύς or also Ὀδυσεύς, Dutch pronunciation: Odíssuis) or **Ulixes** (Latin) is a figure in the classical antiquity myth cycle surrounding the Trojan War. He is the king of the island of Ithaca, son of Laërtes and Antikleia, a cunning Greek captain, inventor of the ruse with the wooden horse through which the war is won after ten years, after which he wanders for another ten years before returning home. He is an important character in Homer's Iliad, while in Homer's Odyssey he is the main character. Other classical poets also wrote about him, such as Sophokles, in the *Philoktetes*. Philosophers liked to draw on the Odysseus from the Iliad, whom they saw as a paragon of perseverance. Poets favored his cunning and were more likely to choose the Odyssey for their Odysseus interpretation.

Experiences

The surviving story of Odysseus as recorded by Homer, in which he encounters all sorts of mythical creatures in his years of wandering in addition to human adversaries, is actually a kind of adventure novel *avant la lettre.*

Trojan War

When Odysseus and Penelope, living on Ithaca have just had their son Telemachos, Menelaus and a group of others, including Palamedes, come to him to persuade him to fight in the Trojan War. Odysseus, not wanting to join after Telemachos' birth, pretends to have gone insane and begins sowing salt in fields. Palamedes, knowing how cunning Odysseus is, does not let himself be fooled, goes to check and puts Telemachos in front of the plow. Odysseus immediately dodges his newborn son, but in doing so betrays himself. Odysseus is persuaded, but makes Penelope promise that if he has not returned by the time Telemachos has a beard, she will choose a new husband.

So Odysseus fought in the Trojan War and received Achilles' armor after his death. Ajax, Telamon's son, did not receive the armor and killed a flock of sheep. Having mistaken these sheep for the Greek captains at the hands of Athena, he wanted to cool his anger and committed suicide. After ten years of fighting, the Greeks realized that they could never take Troy with a siege alone. Odysseus devised a ruse: the Greeks sailed with their men to Tenedos, an island off the coast of Troy, to hide there, but left one of their own, Sinon near Troy with a large wooden structure, the Trojan horse, in which Greek soldiers had hidden. The Trojans think, since the Greeks are gone, that they have given up. Sinon says it is an offering from the Greeks to Athens and that if the Trojans take the horse within their walls, it will ensure peace in Troy. But to do so, they must tear down part of the wall around their city. Kassandra and Laokoön still warn their fellow townsmen that it is a ruse, but nevertheless the Trojans fall into the trap. Sinon, once it is in Troy and night has fallen, opens the horse. The Greeks climb out of the horse and are able to open the city gates and thus conquer Troy, killing many of the inhabitants.

Odysseus already drew the ire of Poseidon on his return journey because he had poked out the eye of Polyphemos, the son of Poseidon. Poseidon therefore promised him that his return journey would not be entirely without problems.

Kikonen

Odysseus, after taking Troy, began his journey back to his island of Ithaca, where his wife Penelope and his son Telemachos were waiting for him. He arrived first on the island of the Kikons. The Kikons were allies of the Trojans during the war, and for this reason Odysseus and his men destroyed the entire island and killed almost all the Kikons except Maron, the priest of Apollo. Maron gave Odysseus twelve jars of intoxicating wine, which would later serve him well. Odysseus had to leave with his men headlong, because some Kikons, who had managed to flee, had returned with associates. He lost six men on each of his ships because of their actions.

Lotus Eaters

Odysseus then made his way to the Cyclades and sailed on to the island of the Lotus Eaters, also called Lotoseters or Lotophagen. The Lotus Eaters, as their name suggests, eat only lotus. Odysseus immediately sent three men here to explore. When these did not return after a certain time, Odysseus and the others decided to search for them. It turned out that the scouts did not want to return home because they had eaten from the lotus. Odysseus dragged the men off the island and ordered the others especially not to eat of the magic flowers. The scouts had to be tied up on the boat as Odysseus sailed away with his men.

The Cyclops Polyphemos

Odysseus then reached the island of Sicily, which at that time was inhabited by cyclopes. Odysseus and his men entered a huge cave filled with racks of cheese and milk, looking as if sheep were kept there. As a gift to the host, Odysseus had brought bags of wine from the priest of the Kikonen. When they had waited a while, the giant cyclops Polyphemos entered the cave with his sheep and asked who the strangers were. Odysseus said his name was "Nobody." Polyphemos was not too friendly and decided to eat some of Odysseus' men. However, as a gift to Odysseus, Polyphemos promised to eat him last. Odysseus wanted to kill the cyclops but realized that he and his men would then be trapped in the cave since they were not strong enough to push away the boulder in front of the entrance. Therefore, he resorted to a ruse.

Every day Polyphemos ate four men, two in the morning and two in the evening, and at one point Odysseus asked if Polyphemos did not want something to drink. He gave Polyphemos the bags of wine, which the

cyclops emptied completely. Then the latter fell into a deep sleep.
Odysseus made a found pole very pointed and heated it in the fire.
Together with four more men, Odysseus stuck this pole into Polyphemos'
one eye, blinding him. Polyphemos then called for the help of other
cyclopes. They asked why Polyphemos called for help, to which he
replied, "No one's trickery, no violence, threatens me with
death!"Odysseus realized that he was not yet out of the cave, because the
only exit was blocked by a large stone, which was impossible to get out. In
the morning, Polyphemos always let the sheep out, and this, according to
Odysseus, was the time to escape. He ordered his men to each hang
under two sheep to get out. For himself, however, only one remained,
under which he went to hang. Polyphemos felt with his hands whether only
the sheep went out through the exit, and thus did not feel that there were
people hanging under the sheep. At the last sheep, which Odysseus was
hanging under, he became suspicious, for this one should be ahead.
Nevertheless, he let him pass. When Odysseus arrived on his ship, he
could not help but shout to Polyphemos that they had escaped. In
response, Polyphemos threw a rock, which only just missed the ship.
Odysseus yelled after Polyphemos that he would prefer to kill him, which
was answered with a second boulder. Polyphemos felt hurt and sought the
help of his father: the god Poseidon. He asked his father if he could make
the rest of Odysseus' journey to Ithaca even more difficult. Because of his
flight, Odysseus had to leave behind his companion Achaimenides, but he
would later be taken by Aeneas.

Aiolos

After sailing for some time, Odysseus arrives on an island, where he finds
Aiolos, the god of wind. Odysseus and his men are well received on his
island and stay there for more than a month in Aiolos' palace. When
Odysseus leaves again, Aiolos gives him a bag, which contains all the
winds except the south wind. Odysseus must on no account open it, for he
must use the winds for his masts: if there is no wind, he can move on
again by opening the sack. His men are naturally curious to know what is
in the sack, but Odysseus does not reveal anything. The men think there
is gold and jewels in the sack, and think Odysseus wants to keep these
treasures for himself. Due to favorable winds from Aeolus, Odysseus and
his men soon approach Ithaca. When the men have almost reached
Ithaca, Odysseus falls asleep due to fatigue. His men toast the
homecoming with wine and open all the bags and so does the bag of all
the winds, and a great storm breaks out, driving them away from Ithaca,
back to the island of Aiolos. The god is very surprised to see Odysseus
again, but when he explains what has happened he realizes that one of
the Olympian gods is antagonizing Odysseus. Moreover, he is angry that

Odysseus has handled his gift in this way, so he immediately expels him and his entourage from his palace.

Laistrygonen

After sailing away from Aiolos, Odysseus and his men reach the island of the Laistrygons. Almost all of Odysseus' ships dock in the harbor, only Odysseus' ship remains at a distance. The Laistrygons are giants and use rocks to crush Odysseus' ships lying in the harbor. Odysseus' ship manages to escape in the nick of time and chased by rocks, they sail to Aiaia, the home of the sorceress Kirke, aka Circe.

Kirke

On Aiaia, Odysseus sends out a group of scouts to see what the island has to offer. However, when they stay away for a very long time, Odysseus decides to look for himself. On his quest, he meets Hermes, the messenger of the gods. He warns Odysseus about the dangerous magic potion of the sorceress Kirke. If Odysseus drinks of this, he will turn into a beast unless he ingests an herb called Moly that Hermes offers him. Odysseus does not trust it because Moly is poisonous. Hermes eventually succeeds in convincing Odysseus. Odysseus eats it, and proceeds to find Kirke's palace. Around the palace, he sees all kinds of different beasts walking. He finds out that his men have also been turned into animals, namely swine.

Odysseus meets Kirke and he orders her to let his men go. Kirke wants to offer him a drink first, and Odysseus drinks it, hoping that Hermes' herb will work. Kirke gets all upset when Odysseus does not turn into an animal, and says she will conjure his men back, if Odysseus goes to bed with her. Odysseus goes to bed with her, and as promised, the animals turn back into men. Odysseus and his men stayed on Aiaia for one year. Then they moved on again.

Underworld

Kirke had advised Odysseus to go to the underworld and seek the shadow of the blind seer Teiresias. With Kirke's help, Odysseus reaches the underworld and enters it alone. He must dig a pit in the underworld and offer three sacrifices there: a mixture of milk and honey, sweet wine and water. Over this he must sprinkle flour, make some vows and sacrifice a black ram and a black sheep. Odysseus had heard from Kirke that Teiresias is the first to be allowed to drink of the blood, but of course all the specters come to the blood, which Odysseus tries to keep at bay with his sword. He sees his mother among the shadows, who was still alive when he left Ithaca, but he is not allowed to let her drink of the blood either until Teiresias has had enough. Teiresias finally turns to Odysseus and he prophesies to him that he and his men will arrive safely at Ithaca if he leaves alone the cows of Helios, the sun god, which graze on the island of Thrinakia. Back home, he will have to kill the suitors who want to marry Penelope, but after that he will have a peaceful old age. The seer also tells Odysseus that Poseidon is the cause of his misfortune. After this prediction, Odysseus was finally able to make his mother drink of the blood. His mother committed suicide because she could no longer bear to live without him. Odysseus also meets Agamemnon, one of the other leaders of the siege of Troy, who tells in what horrible way he died. Odysseus remains in the realm of the dead not a moment longer after meeting his mother and Agamemnon.

He and his crew sailed back to the island of Kirke and left there after a good night's sleep. Odysseus stayed on the island for a total of five days, but what he and his men do not know is that each day in the palace is a year in the real world. When he wants to leave again from the beach of Aiaia, he sees that his ship is under the sand. They have to dig it out first.

Sirens

Sirens are half goddesses, half vulture and half human. They tempt sailors with their singing to sail toward them, causing the ships to run into rocks and perish, leaving the crew to fare badly.

Odysseus had received good advice from Kirke to plug up his ears and those of his men so that they would not be tempted to go to the sirens and dig their own graves. He plugged his men's ears with beeswax, but had himself tied to the mast, so that he could hear the sirens' songs but could not sail toward them. He additionally instructed his men that if he shouted they were not to untie him, but to tie him even more firmly. Thus they passed the island of the sirens unscathed.

Skylla and Charybdis

Odysseus, after passing the sirens in one piece, came with his ship through a narrow strait, presumably the Strait of Messina. They entered a cave and were given a choice: they either had to pass Charybdis, which swallows and spits out water several times a day, risking losing the entire ship, or pass Skylla, a six-headed monster that would kill or take away six of his men. Odysseus chose the latter, preferring to lose six of his men rather than all of them.

Helios

Odysseus arrives at Thrinakia, present-day Sicily, the island where the sun god Helios grazes his cattle. Odysseus would have preferred to avoid this island, given the warnings of Teiresias and Kirke. But they cannot go back, and the men get Odysseus to stay on the island for at least a day. A period of unfavorable weather breaks out, and Odysseus is obliged to stay on the island longer. He has made his men swear to stay away from the cattle, but after a while the food runs out, and the men would rather incur the wrath of the gods than starve to death. They slaughter some cattle and roast them over a fire. Odysseus wakes up, and comes swearing and ranting to the men. Helios forces Zeus to punish the men, and Zeus promises him that they will not escape their punishment.

When the wind has died down, Odysseus and his men are able to leave again. Even before Helios' island is out of sight, a great storm breaks out and Zeus' lightning strikes Odysseus' ship, causing it to sink. All the men drown, only Odysseus remains alive. He will now have to continue his journey back home alone.

Kalypso

Odysseus just barely managed to grab onto a piece of wreckage and floats on. He reaches Charybdis once more, who drains the sea, causing Odysseus to lose his raft. He himself has just managed to grab hold of a branch on an island, and hangs onto it until Charybdis spits out the sea again. He jumps onto the raft and moves on again, without Skylla noticing him.

Odysseus drifts to the mysterious island of Ogygia, where the goddess Kalypso lives with several other women. These women giggle when they see Odysseus, because they have never seen a man before. Odysseus is well cared for on the island, and Kalypso shows him that she does like him. Kalypso tells him to forget Penelope, and that she can make him immortal and eternally young, but she cannot persuade Odysseus to refrain from returning home and to Penelope. However, she does deprive him of all sense of time, and so he thinks he is only on the island for seven days, when in reality he was there for seven years.

Athena thinks Odysseus' stay on Ogygia has been enough after seven
years and persuades Zeus to send Hermes to Kalypso, who orders her to
let Odysseus go. She is unwilling and says that the gods simply cannot
have it that she loves a mortal, moreover, she says that Zeus himself
caused Odysseus to wash up here. In the end, Kalypso lets Odysseus go
and orders him to build a boat with which he can sail home.

The Phaeacians

When Odysseus has the island of the Phaeacians in sight, Poseidon
causes a storm, causing Odysseus to be shipwrecked again. He thinks he
is now going to die, but just at that moment the nymph Ino (aka
Leukothea) appears, telling him that he will reach the island safely if he
does as she says. She instructs him to tie her kerchief, which removes the
fear of doom and death, around his chest and jump naked into the water.
Odysseus doesn't quite trust her, but he has no choice. Except for the
headscarf, he jumps into the water naked and swims to shore. It takes
another two days despite Pallas Athena's help before Odysseus washes
up on shore. There he takes off the headscarf, and, as Ino had instructed
him, throws it back into the sea with his face averted. Then he goes to rest
completely naked in the bushes.

Athena, disguised as a close friend, appears to the Faiaak princess
Nausikaä in a dream. She tells Nausikaä to go to the beach to do her
laundry; she also points out that Nausikaä may be getting married soon.
The next day, Nausikaä and her servants go to do laundry at the beach.
Odysseus wakes to the sounds of Nausikaä and her servants and,
covered with some leaves and a twig in his hand, steps out of the bushes.
All the servants run off, only Nausikaä remains standing. She does not
fear the naked unknown man. Odysseus asks her if she has a cloth for
him to wrap and if she knows the way to the city. Nausikaä orders her
servants to wash Odysseus, but Odysseus prefers to do it himself. When
he is washed, Nausikaä explains to him how to get to the city and how to
act to be received hospitably.

He acts as he is told and goes to the palace. He is rendered invisible by
the goddess Athena and walks straight toward Queen Arete. When he
drops down and hugs her knees, his invisibility disappears, startling the
queen. Odysseus begs Arete to let him go home, and the Phaeacians give
him the best food and stuff because they think Odysseus is a god.
However, Odysseus tells them that he is an ordinary person, and not a
god. King Alkinoös promises him a ship to sail home.

A banquet is held for Odysseus, and Odysseus asks a singer if he can sing about the Trojan War. This song moves Odysseus greatly, and he begins to weep. Alkinoös asks him to reveal his name, as he has now become very curious. Odysseus now replies that he is Odysseus, the man who invented the Horse of Troy. Alkinoös asks him if he can tell about his adventures on the way home, and Odysseus narrates on late into the night.

The Phaeacians eventually bring Odysseus with their ship the final stretch to Ithaca, but according to some readings are severely punished by Poseidon for this: either their ship or their entire island sank into the sea.

Return to Ithaca

During the twenty years that Odysseus is away from home, Penelope gets more and more suitors in his house who want to marry her. Penelope, however, still loves Odysseus and does not want to remarry. They assure her that Odysseus has died and they tell her that she cannot go on living this way. Penelope tells them she will marry someone as soon as she has woven a shroud for Laërtes, Odysseus' old father. She begins working on this shroud, but soon comes to the conclusion that she will be finished with it in a short time. Therefore, she weaves during the day, but removes the shroud at night.

Odysseus wakes up on an island that is strange to him, shrouded in mist. He meets Athena, who tells him that he is really on Ithaca, and to prove it, she removes the fog. Odysseus now recognizes the island and Athena tells him that he cannot go to Penelope right away, because of the suitors. She says that if he went to Penelope now, he would die like Agamemnon. To protect him from that, Athena turns him into a beggar and sends him to Eumaios, the swineherd. Moreover, Athena tells him that she will leave for Sparta to send his son Telemachos back home. This is because he has set out to make inquiries about his father.

In time, Eumaios finds out that the beggar is actually his master and warns him not to return to his palace, at least not until Telemachos has returned. When Telemachos is back on Ithaca, Athena returns Odysseus to his true form. At first Telemachos does not recognize his father, but Odysseus convinces him that it is. Odysseus asks his son to help him defeat the suitors, to which Telemachos naturally agrees.

Odysseus is again transformed into a beggar by Athena and goes to his palace. Meanwhile, the suitors have become very restless and want

Penelope to make a choice now. She invents a ruse, so she does not have to marry anyone. On the wall still hangs Odysseus' bow, which only he can string. She organizes a contest and the one who can string the bow and use it to shoot an arrow through the eyes of twelve axes attached to the top at once becomes the new husband. All the suitors try to string the bow, but none of them succeed. Odysseus, meanwhile, has walked to the palace. Odysseus, still enchanted, asks if he can give it a try. The suitors shout that a beggar can't string a bow at all, but Penelope says the beggar can try too. Odysseus strains the bow and shoots through all 12 eyes with it, so all the suitors are stunned. Odysseus is transformed back into his normal form, so the suitors recognize him and become frightened. They try to kill Odysseus, whereupon he kills one of them. The suitors are indignant and feel they have done nothing wrong. However, they did; they lived off Odysseus' money for years and insulted his wife. After this, Odysseus shoots more of them and a real battle begins. He gets help from Telemachos and together they kill them all. After this gruesome battle, Odysseus orders his old nurse, Eurykleia, to fetch all the unfaithful servants. This she is only too happy to do. The terrified girls are forced to drag out the corpses of the suitors and clean the great hall. Telemachos stretches a stout rope between the roof and the court wall, on which he hangs the unfaithful servants one by one.

Odysseus goes in search of Penelope after the cleanup and is reunited with her. They promise to stay together forever.

Imitation of the figure of Odysseus

Not only the Romans used the figure Odysseus, with "their" Ulixes, to inspire stories or have him play a leading role in them. Even today he appears regularly in books and stories.

In Dantes' *Inferno,* Odysseus burns in hell among evil counselors, as does Diomedes. He tells Dante and Virgil that after all his wanderings he made one last journey, to the mountain of purification on the other side of the earth, where God sank his ship. Odysseus also plays a role in Shakespeare's *Troïlus and Cressida* and James Joyce's *Ulysses* is named after him. He further appears, for example, in the children's book *De vloek van Polyfemos*, written by Evert Hartman.

Fine art

Odysseus appears regularly in ancient and contemporary art. The Greeks already painted him frequently on vases and plates, but painters of the 15th and 16th also painted him on canvases.

Music

Claudio Monteverdi wrote the opera *Il Ritorno d'Ulisse in Patria* in 1641, about the return of Odysseus to Ithaca.At least three "settings" followed in the 20th century, one by John Harbison (*Odysseus*) and one by Nicholas Maw (*Odysseus*). Alan Hovhaness devoted his 25th symphony to the love between Odysseus and Penelope.

Movie

The story of Odysseus and his adventures has been filmed many times, including in the miniseries The Odyssey. A very free interpretation is the 2000 film O Brother, Where Art Thou?

Odyssean construction

The term "Odyssean construction" is sometimes used in government circles, referring to Odysseus' encounter with the Sirens. The years 2002-2004 were characterized by relatively low growth or even decline in tax revenues as well as rising marginal tax rates. In the year 2005, when tax revenues (especially on income and wealth) suddenly skyrocketed, the government's financing deficit narrowed. For the voter and the elected representative of the people, this signals that government finances are in order and thus there is a surplus, the use of which has been released. The call of the voter is compared to the lure of the Sirens who, with their clean singing, managed to seduce many a boatman and set him on the cliffs. For Odysseus, the solution was as simple as it was effective: he had his crewmen tie him to the mast in order to resist the temptation by force.

Orpheus

A legendary musician and poet who attempted to retrieve his dead wife from the Underworld

Orpheus (Ancient Greek: Ὀρφεύς) is a musician, poet and prophet from Greek mythology. According to tradition, he lived in Thrace. Tradition says he could make trees and animals dance with his music. He was famous with the Lyre, and is said to have been taught by Apollo himself.

He is best known for the myth of Orpheus and Eurydice, which has been set to music by many writers and composers. The story tells how Orpheus, after the death of his wife Eurydice, descends to the underworld and negotiates with Hades, god of the underworld, to return his wife to the realm of the living. His singing charms Hades, and he is granted permission to take Eurydice up with him, on the condition that he does not look back once on his upward journey. Of course, just before leaving the underworld, he is so concerned for his wife that he looks back anyway, thus dooming her to the underworld after all.

In antiquity, this semi-mythical figure was regarded as a historical person to whom some poems and philosophical propositions were attributed. His name is associated with the religious-wisdom movement of Orphism. He was even counted by some among the Seven Wise Men.

Orpheus is said to have been killed by nymphs.

Perseus

The son of Zeus, founder-king of Mycenae, and slayer of the Gorgon Medusa

Perseus (Ancient Greek: Περσεύς) is a figure from Greek mythology. He was a heros, son of Zeus and Danaë. Best known for his actions against the Gorgo Medusa.

An oracle told Akrisios, king of the Greek city-state of Argos, that one day he would be killed by his grandson. As a precaution, he had his only daughter Danaë locked in a bronze chamber until she was too old to have children. What Akrisios did not know was that the chief god Zeus had other plans for Argos. Zeus was known for his extramarital affairs with mortal women. But he was never allowed to show himself to a mortal for then the mortal would be struck by lightning. For this reason, but also to get into the bronze room, he transformed himself into a rain of golden dust; he entered through the lattice window and got Danaë pregnant.

Danaë had a son, Perseus. Akrisios had her and her son locked in an empty wooden coffin, which was then thrown into the sea. They washed up on the island of Seriphos, where Diktys, a kind fisherman took them in and cared for them.

Perseus and Medusa

Diktys' lecherous brother Polydektes, king of Seriphos, wanted Danaë as a wife but Perseus defended the honor of his reluctant mother. Enraged by the rejection, Polydektes demanded horses from every inhabitant as a gift for the next suitor, Hippodameia, the daughter of King Oinomaos of Pisa. Perseus had no horses, but said he would get anything for the king, even if it was the head of the Gorgo Medusa. Polydectes knew that no one had ever returned from the Gorgons and sent Perseus on his way.

Zeus asked Athena to help his son. She pointed Perseus to a cave in Libya where three old women lived, the Graeae. They knew where the nymphs were that could give Perseus special weapons against the Gorgons. The Graeae were sisters of the Gorgons and refused to help. Together they had one eye and one tooth. When one passed the eye to another so she could watch the stranger, Perseus snatched the eye and threatened not to give it back until they told him where the nymphs lived. They told him that the nymphs lived by the Styx in the underworld. Perseus then returned the eye. He went to the nymphs who gave him weapons and other items. He was given a bag for Medusa's head and Hades' helmet that rendered invisible. Hermes, the messenger of the gods, gave him a sickle and lent him his winged sandals so that he could quickly flee from her two sisters, Stheino and Euryale (who had golden wings and bronze hands). Hermes also helped him polish the shield so that the shield mirrored, so that Perseus could see the Gorgons in mirror image through his shield and not become petrified like everyone else when he looked at them. There are sources that say Perseus received the mirrored shield from Athena.

Perseus noticed he was getting closer to the Gorgons, as more and more petrified people stood along the road. Invisible through his magic helmet and looking through his shield, Perseus walked toward Medusa. She was hideous, with snakes instead of hair and a red tongue between two large fangs. He beheaded her with one stroke of his sickle, put the head in the bag and flew away. Unable to keep up with him, Stheino and Euryale returned and mourned their sister.

On the way back, Perseus spent the night in the land of the Hesperides, daughters of Atlas. Their garden of golden apples (a wedding gift from Gaia to Zeus and Hera), was strictly guarded by Atlas, to whom had been told that a son of Zeus wanted to steal the apples. He tried to kill Perseus, but Perseus grabbed Medusa's head and petrified him (today's Atlas Mountains).

Perseus and Andromeda

Perseus was flying along the coast of Ethiopia when he saw far below him a young woman chained to a tree on a cliff near the sea. As he got closer, he saw two sad figures on the cliffs, her parents, King Cepheus and Queen Cassiopeia. They told him what had happened.

Cassiopeia had haughtily claimed to be more beautiful than the Nereids, the daughters of Nereus, the Old Man of the Sea and an ancestor of Poseidon. As punishment for this pride (hybris), Poseidon caused the coastal regions of Ethiopia to be ravaged by a sea monster named Cetus. An oracle had told Cepheus that he could make the sea monster leave by sacrificing his daughter Andromeda.

Perseus proposed to the royal couple to save Andromeda in exchange for her hand. At that moment, the sea monster emerged and Cepheus quickly agreed. Perseus killed the monster with his sickle and stripped Andromeda of her chains. That evening, Cepheus announced the marriage between Andromeda and the Greek hero, forgetting that he had already promised her to his brother Phineus. A battle broke out and when Perseus realized that Phineus was well outnumbered with his troops, he grabbed Medusa's head again and thus petrified them.

Perseus sailed with Andromeda to the island of Seriphos. Upon arrival, he discovered that Polydektes was still chasing his mother. He brought Danae and Andromeda to Dictys and headed for the royal palace. There he told them that he had returned with the gift for Hippodameia. He petrified all present by showing the head of Medusa again. Perseus gave the hat, sickle and sandals to the messenger Hermes, who brought everything back to the nymphs in Africa. Perseus gave the head of Medusa to Athena, who attached the terrifying head to her shield (aegis). Perseus decided to return to Argos to demand from Akrisios his share of the inheritance.

Perseus and Akrisios

Despite Perseus' forgiveness, Akrisios, thinking of the prophecy, fled to his friend King Teutamides of Larisa. Hearing this, Perseus left Andromeda and Danaë in Argos and set out to make friends with his grandfather. At that time, King Teutamides was holding games in honor of his birthday father. Perseus did not see Akrisios and decided to wait until that evening's banquet. In the meantime, he would participate in the games, introducing discus throwing. He picked up a metal disc and threw it as far away as possible. Suddenly the disc gave way due to strong winds. By a cruel twist of fate, the disc flew into the crowd, killing Akrisios. The prophecy had come true.

Perseus returned to his mother and wife in Argos, but realized that the gods would not allow him to rule the city of the man he had killed. He traded Argos for nearby Tiryns, which he ruled for many years. He founded several cities in the mountain range the Argolids, including the famous city of Mycenae. Andromeda bore him many children, and his grandson Eurystheus was the last in the Perseus dynasty of Argos.

Theseus

The king of Athens and slayer of the Minotaur

Theseus grew up in Troizen, on the east coast of Peloponnese. His mother Aethra did not know who his father was. She had slept nine months earlier with Poseidon, the god of the sea, and with Aigeus, the king of Athens. The latter told Aethra that should she have a son, she should raise him well into a strong man. Aigeus would put his sword and sandals under a stone, and when Theseus was strong enough to lift the stone, he was to come to Athens.

When Theseus turned eighteen he was able to lift the stone and went to Athens. On his way he encountered all kinds of robbers. The first villain was named Skiron. He lived near the sea. He forced travelers to sit on the edge of a rock and wash their feet. Then he kicked them off and the victims were eaten by the giant turtle who lived under the rock. The second villain was named Procrustes. He offered travelers a place to spend the night, namely his own bed. If the guest was taller than the bed, Procrustes cut off the protruding part. If the guest was shorter than the bed he was stretched. The last one was called Sinis. This one with his awesome strength bent over two giant pine trees and tied a passing traveler to them. Then he released the trees and the victim was torn apart. Theseus made the villains suffer the same fate as their victims: Sinis was torn apart, Skiron was eaten by the turtle and Procrustes stretched until he died.

Meanwhile, Aigeus had married Medea, a seer, and had given birth to a son named Medos. When Medea saw Theseus, she knew that if she didn't do something soon, Theseus would become the heir to the throne instead of her son Medos. She decided to give him a test: Theseus had to kill the bull of Marathon. Theseus succeeded, however, and when he returned Medea decided to kill him at the banquet by making him drink poison. Before Theseus drank, he first cut the flesh with his father's sword. When Aigeus saw this the penny dropped for him. He knocked the cup out of Theseus' hand, who was just about to drink.

Aigeus, however, had one more problem. King Minos of Crete threatened war with Athens. That could only be prevented as long as Athens had fourteen youths, seven boys and seven girls, sailed over every nine years as food for the Minotaur. Theseus was one of the fourteen who made the voyage. His goal was to kill the Minotaur and save the lives of the other Athenian youths. He fell in love in Crete with Ariadne, the daughter of King Minos. Ariadne wanted to help him and gave him the *thread of Ariadne* and a sword. Theseus killed the Minotaur and was able to escape from the labyrinth.

Theseus took Ariadne on the boat and together with the other Athenian boys and girls they sailed toward Athens. They stopped at the island of Naxos and danced a dance there. On the seventh day, Theseus promised Ariadne everything that a married man and woman promise to each other. The next day Theseus left early, leaving Ariadne behind. Ariadne was later taken by Dionysus. This is the most common version of the story, told by writers such as Ovid and Catullus. Another version, for example in the *Bibliotheca*, states that Dionysus had claimed Ariadne for himself after arriving on Naxos and Theseus had to give her up.

Theseus still heard Ariadne's call and was cursed. As a result, he forgot to hoist the white sail. In fact, Theseus had agreed with his father before his journey that - if he survived - he would return with a white sail. Now he was sailing with a black sail. When Aigeus saw the ship with the black sail, he thought Theseus had died. He dropped into the sea after which he died. Theseus became king of Athens as a result. The sea into which Aigeus fell has since been called the Aegean Sea.

Furthermore, according to a little-used version of the story, namely in the *Bibliotheca*, Theseus participated in the Argonaut's journey. He is also said to have participated in the Calydonian hunt. Furthermore, he helped Heracles in the journey to gain possession of the belt of the Amazons, according to Philochoros and other writers cited by Plutarchos.

Later he went back to the Amazons and cheated their queen Antiope. She was the sister of Hippolyte, who had been killed by Heracles. Antiope bore Theseus a son whom she named after her deceased sister Hippolytos.

191

He also helped his good friend Pirithoüs against a Centaur and chessed Helena with him. When they also wanted to play chess with Persephone, Hades became angry and, through a ruse, made them take their seats in the "Seat of Oblivion," which penetrated their bodies and prevented them from getting up.

Heracles saved Theseus, but Lycomedes had already made sure he became king. Theseus then set out for the island of Skyros. The king welcomed him kindly and invited him for a walk. During that walk, he pushed Theseus off a rock into the sea. Theseus drowned in Poseidon's sea. In any case, should Poseidon be his father, he would not have saved him.

Notable women

Arachne

A skilled weaver, transformed by Athena into a spider for her blasphemy

Arachne (Ancient Greek: ἀράχνη - "spider") is a figure from Greek and Roman mythology.

The story is told in Ovid's *Metamorphoses, among others*: Arachne could spin and weave extraordinarily well. Her works were fabulous in beauty and all people admired her works. It seemed that she had been taught by the goddess Athena (Roman: Minerva), but Arachne herself denied this. Athena then disguised herself as an old woman and advised Arachne to beg Athena's forgiveness for her proud words. This, however, Arachne refused. Athena became enraged by the girl's hubris and challenged her, now in her own guise, to compete against her in a weaving contest. Arachne made a perfectly beautiful weave, which aroused great anger in Athena. The goddess thereupon pulled Arachne's piece of work to shreds. She additionally struck Arachne several times on the head. Arachne was so shocked by this that she hanged herself to escape punishment. But Athena, out of pity, revived her and turned her into the spider, who would always dangle from a thread, but who would always weave artfully.

With this myth, Greek mythology explains the origin of the spider's web.

Cassandra

A princess of Troy, who was cursed to see the future but never to be believed

Cassandra or **Kassandra** (Greek: Κασσάνδρα; "she who entangles/confuses men/people") was one of the daughters of Priam, the king of Troy and Queen Hecuba. Cassandra was so beautiful that the god Apollo wanted to share bed with her. Cassandra agreed, but in return wanted the gift of being able to foretell the future. Once Apollo granted her wish, however, Cassandra refused to keep her promise.

Apollo was furious and wanted to punish her. But the gods could not undo a granted gift. Apollo asked her for one last kiss and in doing so spat a curse into her mouth, so no one would believe her when she made a prediction.

Indeed, Cassandra predicted the downfall of Troy several times and was not believed by anyone. Together with Laocoön, she warned, also in vain, against bringing in the horse of Troy.

At the taking of Troy, she took refuge in a statue of Pallas Athena, but Ajax the Lesser cruelly snatched her from it. Then Cassandra was carried off to Mykene by Agamemnon as spoils of war. She warned him of his impending death, but was not believed. He was killed in the bath by his

wife Clytaimnestra with axe blows and a little later Cassandra was
beheaded with the same axe.

Nowadays, the term *cassandra prediction* refers to a prediction of doom
that turns out to be correct after the fact; more specifically, to the
phenomenon that predictions of unavoidable doom are generally not
believed, which places the predictor in the helpless situation of knowing
that disaster is imminent, but not being able to convince others to do what
is necessary to limit the damage.

Helen

Daughter of Zeus and Leda, whose abduction brought about the Trojan War

Helena (Ancient Greek: Ἑλένη, *Helenè*) is a figure from Greek mythology. She is a daughter of the chief god Zeus and Leda. Helena was the most beautiful woman in Greece. Zeus is said to have seduced Leda in the guise of a swan and from the eggs laid by Leda, Helena and Polydeukes (Pollux) were born. This story lives on in the Latin expression *ab ovo*. Zeus supposedly did this because he thought the world was overpopulated and wanted to do something about it through Helena. On the same night that Helena and Polydeukes were conceived, Leda's husband, King Tyndareos, also fathered two children with her: Clytaimnestra and Kastor.

When it came time for Helena to marry, many kings and princes came to ask for her hand, or sent emissaries to do so in their stead. Among them were Odysseus, Menestheus, Aias the Great, Patroclus and Idomeneus, but the favorite was Menelaus, who did not come in person but was represented by his brother Agamemnon. All brought wonderful and expensive gifts, except for Odysseus.

Helena was forced to marry Menelaus, who always followed and supported his brother Agamemnon in everything. With Menelaus she had a daughter, Hermione.

Helena to Troy

The myth goes that a few years later Paris, a Trojan prince, came to Sparta to bring the most beautiful girl in the world. This was Helena. Aphrodite had promised him this, if in return he would choose her as the most beautiful goddess in Paris' judgment, thus incurring the wrath of Athena and Hera.

When Paris visited Helena and Menelaus, they received him very warmly, and with the help of Aphrodite, Helena fell in love with Paris and left her husband, to be with her new lover.

When Menelaus discovered that his wife was gone, he asked his brother Agamemnon for advice. Agamemnon, who had wanted to fight Troy for years, told his brother to declare war. Menelaus called together all the kings and heroes of Greece to begin the Trojan War. A "thousand ships" were launched by the Greeks to get Helen back from Troy. In Christopher Marlowe's Doctor Faustus, Mephistopheles makes Helena appear in exchange for Faustus' soul. When Faust beholds her beauty, he exclaims: "Was this the face that launched a thousand ships?"

After ten years of war, when he had finally entered Troy - through the ruse with the wooden horse - Menelaüs wanted to kill Helena. But when Helena saw Menelaüs, the spell broke and she fell in love with him again. Menelaüs, who could not get it over his heart to kill her, took her back to Sparta and grew old with her.

Helena to Egypt

Another tradition (Stesichoros et al.) has it that not Helena herself, but a shadow resembling her is kidnapped by Paris. The real Helena is kidnapped from Sparta by Hermes and taken to Egypt. The Trojan War (waged for the sake of a phantom) would thus have been utterly pointless. All this is the cruel will of Hera, who tries to thwart Aphrodite (because the latter was voted the most beautiful of goddesses by Paris). After the fall of Troy, Menelaus is not allowed to return home: he wanders the seas for seven years with his crew and the pretend Helena. Eventually they are shipwrecked and stranded on the Egyptian coast. When Menelaus arrives at the palace of the local ruler (who is holding Helena captive to marry her), he meets his real wife. This causes some confusion. When the pretend Helena suddenly goes up in smoke, Menelaus realizes that his wife has been staying in Egypt all this time and thus was *not* adulterous. Together they devise a ruse to escape the Egyptian king Proteus and return to their own Sparta. This version forms the basis of Euripides' tragedy *Helena*. This story of a "virtuous Helen" was deliberately created because the image of an adulterous Helen (as she is portrayed by Homer) was an eyesore to Helen worshipers in Sparta and Argos.

Medea

A sorceress and wife of Jason, who killed her own children to punish Jason for his infidelity

The Roman poet Ovid, in his Metamorphoses, carried Medea's story further. After fleeing Corinth, Medea becomes the wife of Aegeus. He later drives her away after her unsuccessful attempt to poison his son, Theseus.

Medea (Latin) or **Medeia** (Ancient Greek: Μήδεια) in Greek mythology was a sorceress from Colchis who helped Jason conquer the Golden Fleece. He took her to Greece, but abandoned her for the daughter of the king of Corinth, after which Medea took gruesome revenge by killing their two sons as well as the king of Corinth and his daughter.

Pedigree

Medea was the daughter of the Oceanid Eidyia and Aietes, the king of Colchis. Through her father, she was a granddaughter of Helios and a niece of the sorceress Circe. Like her, Medea possessed great magic powers.

Medea and Jason

In Colchis was located the Golden Fleece. Jason and the Argonauts came from Iolcus with their ship, the Argo, to retrieve the Golden Fleece by order of King Pelias. However, Aietes, the king of Colchis, had no intention of relinquishing it. But his daughter Medea fell in love with Jason and decided to help him get it anyway. In return, he promised to make her his wife and take her with him to Greece. Thanks to Medea's magic tools, Jason managed to accomplish the impossible tasks Pelias had given him and also managed to defeat the dragon guarding the Golden Fleece and obtain the fleece.

With the Golden Fleece and Medea, Jason and the Argonauts set sail for Greece again. According to some sources, Medea had murdered her half-brother Absyrtus, cut him into pieces and thrown him into the sea, to throw off pursuers who would want to recover the corpse.

According to Apollonius Rhodius, who described in detail in his *Argonautica* the outward and return journeys of the Argonauts, they married in the palace of Alcinoüs, king of the Phaeacians. Alcinoüs, who was threatened by the pursuers from Colchis, had agreed to hand over Medea unless it turned out that she was married to Jason. Alcinoüs' wife Arete had relayed this message to Jason and Medea, who thereupon hastily married. Alcinoüs then resisted Aietes' troops, and Jason and Medea reached Iolcus after some adventures.

Jason had undertaken the Argonaut journey to obtain the throne of Iolcus, but when he returned with the Golden Fleece, Pelias refused to relinquish the throne. Medea took revenge on him. She slaughtered an old ram, cut it into pieces, threw it into a cauldron of boiling water and added all kinds of magic herbs. After some time, a young lamb jumped out of the cauldron. The daughters of Pelias, witnessing this miracle, asked Medea to rejuvenate their father as well. She agreed, and at her insistence the daughters killed their father and threw him into the cauldron. But Medea allowed Pelias to remain dead.

According to some sources, Medea may have previously applied a rejuvenating cure to Jason's father Aeson: Ovid described in his *Metamorphoses* (7, 159-293) how Medea proceeded and replaced Aeson's blood with magic juice that made him 40 years younger.

Jason fled with Medea to Corinth. There they had two sons, the twins Mermeros and Pheres (sometimes called Thessalos and Alkimenes), and, according to some sources, a third named Tissandros. After ten years, however, Jason fell in love with Creüsa (or Glauce), the daughter of the king of Corinth. By marrying her, he could later become king of Corinth. When the king agreed to the marriage, Jason tried to induce Medea to voluntarily renounce any further continuation of their marriage. He claimed that he wanted to marry the Corinthian king's daughter in order to give their sons a good future. Although Medea was deeply offended, Jason pressed ahead with his wedding plans. Medea pretended to consent to the wedding and had Jason's bride-to-be delivered a wedding dress impregnated with a deadly substance. When Creüsa put on the robe, the poison burned into her body, releasing flesh and skin from her bones. Her father Creon, who came to her aid, was also consumed by the fire. Then Medea killed her own children with a sword. With a dragon chariot sent to her by her grandfather Helios, Medea fled. The episode about Medea's revenge on Jason forms the substance of Euripides' famous tragedy *Medea*.

However, there was also a version by the Athenian playwright Karkinos, in which Medea did not kill her children, but hid them from Jason's revenge. This version is mentioned by Karkinos' contemporary Aristotle, and in 2004 it was found on a papyrus fragment in the Louvre.

Medea and Aegeus

After her flight from Corinth, Medea went to King Aegeus in Athens. She had managed to gain his trust by promising to give him back the strength of his youth. She married him and they had a son Medus. To protect Medus' interests, she undertook an attempt to kill Theseus, Aegeus' son from a previous relationship, with poison. When this came to pass, Medea was driven out of the country with her son. According to some sources, she fled to her hometown of Colchis. There her father Aietes had been dethroned by his brother Perses. Medea killed Perses and helped her father regain power. After her death, she was worshiped as a deity by the Colchians.

Medusa

A mortal woman transformed into a hideous gorgon by Athena

Medousa (Ancient Greek: Μέδουσα) or **Medusa** (Latinized) is a monstrous chthonic figure from Greek mythology. Medusa is the daughter of Phorcys and Ceto and is the most famous of the three Gorgons.

Medusa once had a special beauty. However, to her sorrow, she lived in a land where the sun never shone. Medusa begged Athena to let her leave for sunny regions. Athena did not allow this because she feared that people would praise not her, but Medusa for her beauty.

In another version of the myth, Medusa is said to have incurred the wrath of Athena because Poseidon had raped her in Athena's temple. The enraged Athena retaliated by turning Medusa's beautiful hair into a pile of writhing snakes. Furthermore, anyone who looked Medusa in her eyes would instantly turn to stone. Since then, it was her job to petrify as many people as possible. Her sisters begged Athene to change her back. They said, "Let us be like her again!", and so it happened, for Pallas Athene changed them too into Gorgons, and then gave them eternal life.

She was eventually killed and beheaded by the hero Perseus, who was aided in this by Athena and others. From her blood (as a result of an earlier love with Poseidon) were born the winged horse Pegasus and the giant Chrysaor. With the head, Perseus petrified a sea monster and an entire army, and the king who ordered him to kill Medusa. Eventually her head was given by Perseus to Athena, who placed it on her shield to petrify enemies with.

Pandora

In Greek mythology, **Pandora** (Ancient Greek: Πανδώρα) (her name can mean both *bearer of all gifts* and *giver of all gifts* or *gifted*) is the name of the first woman, who was formed by Hephaistos from water and earth. She was sent by Zeus to mortals as a punishment to bring calamity upon them after Prometheus stole fire from the sky, with the purpose of redeeming men from their unfortunate condition.

Myth

Prometheus and his brother Epimetheus had been commissioned by *Zeus* to make man. So they made man, but because the man was so unhappy, Prometheus stole a burning torch from the Olympos and gave mankind the fire. Zeus thought this betrayal was so bad that he wanted to punish mankind. In order not to offend Prometheus and Epimetheus, he did not do so directly. He ordered Hephaistos to form from water and earth a woman named Pandora. Then all the gods bestowed good gifts on her. Athena gave her intelligence, talent and manners. She dressed her in the most beautiful and colorful clothes. Aphrodite gave her the grace and beauty of a goddess. The other gods gave her gold and put flowers in her hair. The last god, Hermes, gave her speech and planted shameless thoughts and a deceitful nature in her being. This gave her a trait that no other mortal had: curiosity.

Zeus gave her to Prometheus, but the latter knew that a gift from the gods is not without consequences and refused her. He advised his brother to do the same. Zeus thereupon had Hermes bring her to Epimetheus, Prometheus' foolish brother. Notwithstanding Prometheus' warnings, he took her as his wife. Zeus also gave the couple a *pithos* (vessel), in which all accidents were locked. If the vessel remained closed, they could not affect anyone. Pandora was curious and wanted to open the vessel, but Epimetheus stopped her. One day Pandora could not contain her curiosity and opened the vessel, freeing all the disasters, diseases and worries that were spreading over the earth: man's carefree existence had come to an end.

Pandora shut the lid startled, with the result that *hope* could not escape. Hence, among the fiercest disasters that plague people on earth, hope alone remains. Hope is sometimes represented as the bird that flew out of the vessel when it was opened for a second time, as a message of consolation to humans (humanity, ape species).

According to another, pessimistic version, however, hope is the only thing people are deprived of. A third interpretation implies that hope itself is also a poisoned gift. After all, hope for something else is non-acceptance of what is manifested here and now.

Pandora gave her consort several daughters, Prophasis, the goddess of subterfuge, Metameleia, the goddess of repentance and Pyrrha, who later became the wife of Deukalion.

Polyxena

The youngest daughter of the king of Troy, sacrificed to the ghost of Achilles

Polyxena (Greek: Πολυξένη) in Greek mythology is the youngest daughter of King Priam of Troy and Hecuba, and thus a sister of Hector, Paris, Deïphobus, Helenus, Troïlos and of Creüsa and Cassandra. She is not mentioned by Homer, but according to later descriptions of the Trojan War by authors such as Dares Phrygius, Dictys Cretensis and Hyginus, she was as beautiful as Helena and had long blond hair, and the Greek Achilles fell in love with her. Her parents gave Achilles permission to marry her, after which Hecuba ambushed Achilles and had Paris kill her.

Much-described is the cruel manner in which Polyxena perished at the taking of Troy by the Greeks. According to the *Cypria* (one of the Cyclic epics), she was wounded by Odysseus and Diomedes at the taking of Troy and was buried by Achilles' son Neoptolemus (schol. Eur. *Hec.* 41). However, all later versions of the myth, beginning with Ibycus (fr. 36) and Euripides' play *Hecuba*, tell that she was killed by Neoptolemus. According to Euripides and Seneca (in his *Trojan Women*), the spirit of Achilles appeared over his grave some time after his death and demanded the girl's sacrifice, and according to Ovid (*Metamorphoses* XIII, 439 ff.), the spirit appeared to Agamemnon and his companions with that request. Euripides, who devoted much of his tragedy *Hecuba* to the death of Polyxena, describes the girl being fetched by a tough and decided Odysseus, who must defend himself against the bitter reproaches of her mother Hecuba. In his description, Ovid emphasizes the courage with which Polyxena enters death, stirring even Neoptolemus to tears. In the description of the story by Quintus Smyrnaeus in his *Posthomerica* (XIV, 193-351), Polyxena's sacrifice is necessary to provide good wind for the Greeks to sail back (just as Iphigenia's sacrifice was necessary on the way out).

207

Kings

Agamemnon

A king and commander of the Greek armies during the Trojan War

Agamemnon, sometimes rendered as *Agamemnoon*, (Ancient Greek: Ἀγαμέμνων) is a figure from Greek mythology. He is the son of Atreus, king of Mycenae, and Airope. Agamemnon had a brother, Menelaos, and a sister, Anaxibia.

In the Trojan War, which was fought for Menelaus, Agamemnon was an army commander. Agamemnon was married to Clytaimnestra, the half-sister of Helena (Menelaus' wife, who was in Troy with Paris).Helena describes her brother-in-law in book three of Homer's *Iliad* as a "mighty ruler, a good king and a powerful lance fighter. Agamemnon was not only king of Mycenae, but also commanded much of the Peloponnese. In doing so, he was king over the sea, as he had the largest share of ships in the war against the Trojans. Not for nothing was Agamemnon βασιλευτατος πάντων, "the most kingly of all.

Until the moment Hektor kills Patroclus, the main theme of the *Iliad* is the quarrel between Agamemnon and Achilles. When Agamemnon takes from Achilles the slave girl Briseis, the gift of honor to Achilles, the latter becomes enraged. He no longer wants to fight in the war against Troy. Later in the book, Agamemnon tries to persuade Achilles to fight again by promising him immense gifts. Achilles, however, wants nothing of this.

In 1876, archaeologist Heinrich Schliemann, who would later "discover" Troy, found a golden mask supposedly representing King Agamemnon,

the "Mask of Agamemnon. It was later revealed that the mask predated
the time in which Agamemnon is said to have lived.

Agamemnon had promised the goddess Artemis to sacrifice the finest he
caught while hunting. He did not, and so Artemis allowed an unfavorable
wind to rise so that the Greeks could not leave for Troy. To get an
unfavorable wind anyway, he had to sacrifice his daughter, Iphigeneia,
under pressure from the army. His wife, Clytaimnestra, was furious.
According to another story, Agamemnon went hunting just before leaving.
One of the deer he killed turned out to be one of the sacred hinds of
Artemis. Then, when he also claimed to be better at hunting than Artemis,
the goddess caused a lull in the wind, preventing the Greeks from sailing
to Troy.

During the war, which left Agamemnon away from home for years,
Klytaimnestra began a relationship with Aigisthos, son of Thyestes (i.e.
Agamemnon's cousin). When Agamemnon returned victorious from Troy,
including the Trojan princess Kassandra as the spoils of war, Aigisthos
killed him in the bath. Another story suggests that Aigisthos persuades
Klytaimnestra to kill Agamemnon in that same bath.

Agamemnon and Clytaimnestra had four children: Iphigeneia, Electra,
Chrysothemis and Orestes. Chrysothemis did not play an important role in
Greek mythology and is therefore often omitted. The other three children
carried the Tantalos curse (see below) further into their lives. Electra and
Orestes avenged their father by killing their mother and her lover.

The Tantalos genus

Agamemnon, together with his brother Menelaus and his cousin Aigisthos,
forms the fourth generation of the Tantalos family (see image). The
lineage was constantly tormented by punishments from the gods, the
cause of which also lay with the gods themselves.

Tantalos, the progenitor, was a wealthy king in Asia Minor and lived on
equal terms with the gods. He wanted to test their omniscience and invited
the gods to a dinner for which he killed his own son Pelops and served it
to them. All the gods refused to eat, except Demeter, who, out of sorrow
for her daughter being in the underworld, did not have her mind so much
about it, and ate a piece of Pelops' shoulder. Pelops was then revived and
given an ivory shoulder.

The gods punished Tantalos in the Tartaros with the famous "Tantalus torment"; always tied up, starving and thirsty, with water just barely reaching his mouth and apples hanging above him just out of reach.

Tantalos had a daughter, Niobe. The latter insulted Leto (the mother of Apollo and Artemis) with the fact that Leto had only two children and she had fourteen. Apollo and Artemis avenged their mother for this insult. Artemis killed all of Niobe's daughters and Apollo killed all of her sons.

Pelops also had two sons, Thyestes and Atreus. Both sons fought for the throne a number of times. In the end, it was Atreus who held out.

Atreus had two sons: Agamemnon and Menelaus. Agamemnon became king of Mycenae, Menelaus of Sparta.

Midas

A king of Phrygia granted the power to turn anything to gold with a touch

Midas was a legendary king of Phrygia. Several myths about him are known in Greek mythology. Although he and his father Gordias have remained known primarily from myths, they are believed to be historical figures. According to several writers, Midas' mother was the goddess Cybele.

Golden touch

Because he had saved the drunken satyr Silenos, Dionysos, the wine god, granted him the power to turn everything he touched into gold. However, when his food and child also turned into gold, he decided to wash away the power he had in the river Paktolos.

Donkey ears

Another myth tells that he was a great worshipper of Pan, the god of shepherds and rugged lands. But by siding with Pan, he offended Apollo, the god of music.

Pan enjoyed playing simple tunes on his reed flute. Because many people thought it sounded beautiful, he began to boast that he was a better musician than Apollo. He challenged Apollo to a contest in which the mountain god Tmolos had to give a verdict. Tmolos dressed himself as a judge, a wreath of oak foliage on his hair, and bunches of acorns hanging down his face, and listened to the music. Pan began, and everyone was charmed by his cheerful flute pieces. Then Apollo picked up his lyre, and his tones rocked like waves on the gentle breeze, smooth and delightful. Tmolos gave the prize to Apollo. Midas protested and said he liked Pan better.

"You couldn't possibly have heard that," said Tmolos. "There is nothing wrong with my ears" said Midas. At that moment Apollo could no longer control his anger and said, "If you use them this way, you are not worthy of having the ears of a human being." He gave Midas a pair of long, gray and hairy ears, saying, "Now you look like the donkey you are." Midas was ashamed of his new ears and tried to hide them under a turban. After a while, his barber discovered the secret. The barber dared not tell anyone about Midas' deformity, but was also unable to keep it all to himself. So he walked out into the countryside, dug a hole and whispered his secret to the earth. Every secret, however, wants to become public. Where the barber had dug the hole, a grove of reeds grew, and when the wind blew through it, it rustled and seemed to shout, "King Midas has donkey ears! King Midas has donkey ears!" When Midas discovered that everyone knew about his secret, he died of shame.

Cause of death

In mythology, in addition to "death by shame," there is also talk of being poisoned with bull's blood.

Tomb mound

The so-called "Tomb Mound of King Midas" at Gordion is currently identified as the tomb of his father Gordias. It is not known what happened to his body after Midas' death.

Oedipus

A king of Thebes fated to kill his father and marry his mother

Oidipous (Ancient Greek: Οἰδίπους) or **Oedipus** (Latinized), formerly in Dutch also **Edipus**, is a figure from Greek mythology. Oedipus is a son of Laios (king of Thebes) and Iokaste.

Oedipus is the main character in Sophokles' tragedy *King Oedipus* (*Oidipous tyrannos* or *Oedipus Rex*) from 430 B.C. and in his *Oidipus at Kolonos*. Furthermore, he figures in Euripides' *Phoinissai*. Aeschylos (*Seven against Thebes*) and Aristophanes also write poems about Oedipus and his progeny. However, the myth of Oedipus is much older than these 5th century BCE playwrights: already Homer makes a sideways allusion to the Oedipus legend.

Myth

In the Oedipus myth, the Oracle promised King Laios a long-awaited heir but at the same time warned that he would perish at the hands of his own child. To prevent this, the king would dispose of his newborn son. He cut the tendons in his infant son's feet (Oedipus literally means *swollen feet*) and ordered the keeper of the royal flock to take the child to the mountains and leave him there. However, the shepherd who had to leave the baby behind could not bring himself to do such a thing. In the mountains, he gave the baby to a shepherd friend from neighboring Corinth. The latter brought the child to the childless royal couple Polybus and Periboea where Oedipus grew up as their son and heir. Later, Oedipus heard from the Oracle that he would kill his father (whom, however, he did not know) and marry his mother. Fearing this, he thereupon fled Corinth.

While wandering, he unknowingly encounters his biological father at a crossroads in a region called Fokis. As Oedipus approaches the crossroads, he sees a herald escorting a traveling chariot approaching him. The herald violently forces him off the road and Oedipus, in blind rage, slaps the man. The distinguished traveler in the chariot smacks him on the head with his cane. Immediately Oedipus strikes back, causing the man to tumble backwards out of the chariot. He kills the entire retinue; only one servant is able to escape.

Later he passes through Thebes, which is terrorized by a sphinx after the king's death. This sphinx kills anyone who cannot solve the given riddle. The riddle reads, "What creature walks on four legs in the morning, two in the afternoon and three in the evening?"

Oedipus manages to solve the riddle: a man "walks" as a baby on all fours, as an adult on two legs, and when he has grown old he walks on three legs, two legs and a cane. This is how he delivers the city from the monster. He is crowned king (still unaware that he killed his father, the previous king) and gets the queen (Iocaste, his mother) as his wife. Oedipus fathered four children by his mother, two sons, Eteocles and Polynices, and two daughters, Ismene and Antigone.

Later, when Thebes is ravaged by the plague, the oracle reveals that this is due to an unpunished murderer. Through the blind seer Tiresias, it is learned that this is Oedipus himself. The hapless Oedipus gouges himself and goes wandering as penance. At least in Sophokles' version. In Seneca, we read that the oracle of Delphi alludes not only to parricide but also to incest with the mother. Oedipus, however, does not understand the hints. Tiresias and his daughter Manto must bring help. They perform a sacrifice, but when nothing goes as expected (the peculiarities should be read as allusions to Oedipus' future fate), it is decided to summon Laios from the underworld. The latter openly accuses his son, but still Oedipus does not see what is going on. Only when an old Corinthian and the shepherd Porbas tell him frankly that Iocaste is not only his wife, but also his mother, does it become clear to him. Oedipus pokes his eyes out in response. With Sophokles he calms down after this, in other versions he rages on: he curses nature and believes he has triumphed over fate by his atrocity.

Oedipus is exiled from Thebes and wanders around until he finally arrives at the temple of the Erinyes at Colonus. King Theseus of Athens protects him and he also wins the sympathy of the gods. Meanwhile, his sons Eteocles and Polynices rule by rotation. This degenerates into a power struggle when Eteocles refuses to relinquish the throne and Polynices tries

to find allies abroad to march against Thebes (Seven against Thebes).
Now the Thebans desperately want Oedipus back. Creon and Eteocles try
to persuade Oedipus to return, but the latter refuses. Soon after, Polynices
tries the same thing, first by persuasion and later by force. Oedipus
refuses to return and curses his sons: may they perish by each other's
hand in fratricidal combat. Oedipus passes away peacefully, now
reconciled with the Erinyes who had now become Eumenides for him.

Sisyphus

Sisyphos (Ancient Greek: Σίσυφος) or **Sisyphus** (Latin) is a figure from Greek mythology. He was the founder and king of Corinth and married to the Pleiad Merope. He was a cunning man, but committed the mistake of challenging the gods. He managed to escape from them each time, but in doing so compounded his ultimate punishment. It was that he had to push a boulder against a mountain in the Tartarus until the end of time.

Myth

Sisyphos founded Corinth and promoted trade, but he was also a master of trickery and deceit. He violated the principles of hospitality by killing guests when he thought it would benefit him, seduced his own niece, and deposed his brother as king.

Sisyphos thereby incurred Zeus' wrath by betraying to the river god Asopos that his daughter Aegina had been cheated by Zeus as his umpteenth conquest. He did this because he believed he was on par with the gods and thus could afford to betray a god. This challenge aroused the anger of all the gods.

When Sisyphos died, the gods sent Thanatos (Death) upon him to capture him, chain him, and bring him to the Tartaros. The cunning Sisyphos saw the mood and managed to trick Thanatos. He asked Thanatos to demonstrate how the chains worked and managed to tie him up during this "demonstration. As a result, no one on Earth died. Ares, irritated that his opponents did not die more, freed him a few days later.

Sisyphos was summoned by the gods to really die after this trick, but before Ares and Thanatos came to get him, he instructed his wife not to bury him, and furthermore not to put a coin (obool) under the tongue for the ferryman Charon, so that then he would not be able to cross the Styx to the underworld. Arriving in the underworld, he complained to Hades and Persephone about his wife's negligence, so Hades had no choice but to send him back to complete the necessary rituals. According to other readings, he managed to convince Hades and Persephone that he had been sent to Tartaros by mistake, upon which they released him.

However, Sisyphos did not think of returning and he decided to live on for some time. Finally, the gods sent the swift Hermes upon him, who brought him back to the Tartaros. Thus the gods got hold of him after all and he was condemned in the Tartaros to push a heavy boulder up a steep mountain, which, however, rolled back into the depths from the top each time so that he was doomed to eternally push that boulder up the steep mountain again and again. With this, Zeus showed that in the end the gods were still smarter than Sisyphos, and the latter was punished for his pride.

www.ingramcontent.com/pod-product-compliance
Lightning Source LLC
Chambersburg PA
CBHW071739150726
47998CB00005B/1715